The Fantastic Anatomist

COSTERUS NEW SERIES 126

Series Editors:
C.C. Barfoot, Theo D'haen
and Erik Kooper

The Fantastic Anatomist

A Psychoanalytic Study of Henry James

Ronnie Bailie

 Amsterdam-Atlanta, GA 2000

ISBN 90-420-1581-0

© Editions Rodopi B.V.
   Amsterdam - Atlanta, GA 2000

Printed in The Netherlands

For Thomas Freeman MD

Acknowledgements

I would like to express my gratitude to my editor, Dr C.C. Barfoot of the University of Leiden, for the considerable skill and patience he has brought to the improvement of my manuscript. My other great debt is to the many psychoanalysts and psychotherapists from whose experience and knowledge I have been able to learn in the past decade.

Contents

1	Introduction	1
2	Preliminary Investigation "Theodolinde"	8
3	Case History "A Most Extraordinary Case" "The Jolly Corner"	35
4	Autopsy *The Turn of the Screw*	57
5	The Jameses and Psychoanalysis	84

Appendix   107
"The Case of George Dedlow"

Bibliography   121

Index   125

1

Introduction

> ... as however nobly thinking and feeling creatures, we are abjectly shut up in our material organs. We flutter away from that account of ourselves, on sublime occasion, only to come back to it with the collapse of our wings ...
>
> Henry James, "Is There a Life After Death?"

On the face of it, the fiction of Henry James offers so little of anatomical interest that any attempt to place the body at the heart of an interpretation of his work is more likely to provoke amusement or derision than critical sympathy. For decades, critics have not only observed the relative absence of avowed sexuality from the fiction but have also noted a concomitant of this: that in James much of the general physical apparatus that supports the social life of man is nowhere to be found. Of this trend, the question that his friend Edith Wharton addressed to the novelist himself may be taken as representative:

> "What was your idea in suspending the four principal characters in *The Golden Bowl* in the void? What sort of life did they lead when they were not watching each other? Why have you stripped them of all the *human fringes* we necessarily trail after us through life?"[1]

---

[1] Edith Wharton, *A Backward Glance* (1934), London, 1987, 191.

There is little point in trying to answer this question — and the baffled yet subdued critical animus that hides in it — with a solemn recitation of the details of, say, the physical liaison of the Prince and Charlotte in *The Golden Bowl*. For the implied objection is essentially unanswerable: it is a *fact* that, as James matures, the physical life of his characters is allowed to impinge less and less on their experience. And, for a given character, this is true both of the external world and of persons and material things and of the internal world of impulse and desire. The core of the Jamesian character's experience is ostensibly mental: the thrills and excitements are those of curiosity and stimulated thought, and the body is the poor living servant, the mere vessel of these.

Not all of those who in the novelist's lifetime descried this growing artistic eccentricity had the tact of the ever-kind Edith Wharton. The most determined and unflinching of Henry's early critics was his brother William, whose own characteristic directness was exasperated to find its living anti-type in a younger brother. As William jestingly put it, his brother's purpose was apparently

> to arouse in the reader ... the illusion of a solid object, made (like the "ghost" at the Polytechnic) wholly out of impalpable materials, air, and the prismatic interference of light, ingeniously focussed by mirrors upon empty space.[2]

A practical man, William concludes his epistolary satire with some clear advice to his errant sibling, advice that seems to echo back down the years to another time and another place:

> Say it *out*, for God's sake, ... and have done with it .... The bare perfume of things will not support existence.

And, in fact, *The Golden Bowl* does not even represent the extreme case of this attenuation of the actual, this "terrible denudation" that James, in another context, urged against Hawthorne. That doubtful laurel belongs to *The Sacred Fount*.

---

[2] *The Letters of William James*, ed. Henry James, 2 vols, London, 1920, II, 277-78.

There the whole physical setting of the action and the identities and assigned values of the actors have retained only a minimal, purely emblematic quality. At Newmarch, for a single impossible day, James's imagination allows itself a rare sport. There it breathes a sigh of relief, temporarily liberated from the need to give itself life through plausibly embodied fictions. Or almost liberated, for a minimal fictional situation is retained, but bearing only the aftertaste of physical life, the substance of a geometrical exercise. The house and its ample gardens inhabit an imaginary landscape and, on this Prospero's island, invisible servants tend lights and fires with tireless soundless amenity, or set ambrosial fare before ferociously deliberating phantoms. This is obviously an extreme case, but the alleged absence of the physical from James's work is no critical heresy, nor the delusive fruit of a superficial view. On the contrary, the minutest observation confirms it and it is supported by a compelling internal logic in his development.

For it is only when seen as part of the novelist's inner history that this supremely Jamesian chasm accumulates real interest. In James, the physical is not merely absent — it is *excluded*, and not even his avid life-long emulation of a Balzac is enough to lure it back. The peculiar reality he presents is, with all its characteristic omissions and emphases, presented purposively. Which brings us back to Edith Wharton, and James's reply to her question. What struck her first was her companion's visible alarm at the great lacuna, the missing world she had suddenly conjured up before him. He did not know he had done this thing:

> I saw that my question, instead of starting one of our absorbing literary discussions, had only turned his startled attention on a peculiarity of which he had been completely unconscious.[3]

I have spoken of a reality purposively presented, but, clearly, the purpose that dictated this Great Omission was not one that the most self-conscious of novelists had deliberately entertained. It was the work of an agency that had eluded his attention and discretely declined to accept his control. When Edith Wharton

---

[3] *A Backward Glance*, 191-92.

talks of James being "unconscious", she means only that James was unaware. But it is worth at least considering the possibility that what we are dealing with is a purpose hatched in what James (in his "Preface" to *The American*) called "the deep well of unconscious cerebration". If the purpose in question is in the technical, Freudian sense an "unconscious" one, this may mean that it had become unavailable to consciousness by being repressed.

Now all repressions are, in one way or another, unsuccessful. Of a successful repression we can have, by definition, no knowledge. For there operates in psychical life a phenomenon that Freud called the "return of the repressed"[4], the phrase serving to highlight the unremitting attempt that repressed material makes to be readmitted to consciousness. In fact, the whole symptomatology of psychoneurotic illness is just such a return into a visible (if disguised or converted) form of energies and ideas originally banished from consciousness. What can we say therefore of a fiction that has repressed the body, but that it is likely to be haunted by the body that it has repressed? To this view, the character of James's fiction is best represented emblematically by allusion to the work of Edgar Allan Poe. James was fond of the metaphor of the "house of fiction": it was to him a figurative representation of the seat of the novelist's industry. In the "Preface" to *The Portrait of a Lady* the imaginary house is inhabited by a watcher, a perceiving consciousness, a disembodied spirit who creates. (In the main text this invites further — and invidious — comparison with the dark "habitation" of Osmond's "beautiful mind".) I like to think that the heart of the discarded body beats still under the floor of the Jamesian house of fiction, and that the same body, like the disfigured alternative self of "The Jolly Corner", paces the boards at night. However that may be, I shall try to show that the secret resurgence of the body that is banished from James's work is a crucial determinant of that work.

I am happy to confess that I am not the first to be led into this land of the unlikely, not the first to be intrigued by matters of anatomical import in James's fiction. A footnote in the work of

---

[4] Sigmund Freud, "Repression" (1915), in *The Complete Psychological Works of Sigmund Freud*, 24 vols, ed. James Strachey, London, 1953-74, XIV, 154-56.

Edmund Wilson prodded my imagination a decade ago.[5] And other critics have seen more than they cared, perhaps, to spell out. Of great interest, for example, are some of E.M. Forster's remarks on Jamesian characters:

> They are incapable of fun, of rapid motion, of carnality, and of nine-tenths of heroism. Their clothes will not take off, the diseases that ravage them are anonymous, like the sources of their income .... Maimed creatures can alone breathe in Henry James's pages — maimed yet specialized. They remind one of the exquisite deformities who haunted Egyptian art in the reign of Akhnaton — huge heads and tiny legs, but nevertheless charming. In the following reign they disappear.[6]

This is a few years earlier (1927) than Edith Wharton's memoir (1934) and offers interesting points of comparison with it. But it arrives at a very different conclusion, or, as James would say, comes up in a different place. Forster does not develop his thought minutely, but the implied suspicion is clear and thoroughly illuminating. It is, that the rarified physicality of late Jamesian characters does not mark a supercession of the physical but rather a variety of it. The absence of the physical is not, as it were, a pure deletion, a gap in the orders of being, but is itself constitutive of a mutant species of physicality. In short, James may have renounced the physical but the physical declined to reciprocate.

There would be some distortion in annexing Forster's to a frankly psychoanalytic point of view and I do not propose to attempt it. His talk of maimed creatures may steal a glance at his recently-dead fellow practitioner, but he is really engaged in an imaginative description of James's characters. The fact is, however, that the secret body that insists in James's fiction — in spite of the forces of repression — is indeed a maimed and questionable body. Which brings me to the word "fantastic" in my title. If James's fiction secretly dwells on the body, and if the

---

[5] See "The Ambiguity of Henry James", in Edmund Wilson, *The Triple Thinkers*, New York, 1952.

[6] E.M. Forster, *Aspects of the Novel*, London, 1927, 147.

source of this "unconscious cerebration" lies indeed in his own physical being, this is not to say that the body that haunts the fiction is the same as the body of clinical fact. History assures us that Henry James had one of these. It was born in 1843 and died in 1916. It suffered a back injury in the spring of 1861 and constipation thereafter. For perhaps a decade, it chewed beyond reason. Bearded from 1865, it met the new century beardless. It knew typhoid and jaundice. In 1911 it was treated by James Jackson Putnam in Boston and Dr Joseph Collins in New York. After death, its face resembled that of Napoleon. This is indeed the body of the novelist but it is not that of the fiction. The body in question there is rather the one which Henry James imagined for himself, the body unconscious fantasy substituted for that given him by nature. Beneath varying disguises, it is always this imaginary body that we encounter in the fiction.

A great creative artist does not ransack heaven and hell for something to write about. (As F.R. Leavis once remarked, he does not even write *about*.) That artist is no artist who must actively search for a theme. To say that at bottom he obeys a kind of necessity is to push the case too far in the direction of melodrama. The essential thing is that he does not wholly choose and that he is written as much as he writes. For no man could ever contrive fiction who must, by sheer native wit, assemble that fiction from the degree zero of a bare, unfurnished, unassisted imagination. "He alone shines in Art", says Mann, "whom Eros instructs".[7] For one committed to a psychoanalytic viewpoint, the assisted or instructed imagination is one that elaborates unconscious fantasy into words. This is not to suggest that the conscious and reasonable ego has no place in the creative process, but its contribution comes after the fact, rather in the manner of the process of secondary revision that rounds off the production of a dream.

As a novelist, Henry James's surface material was always the ordinary and more-or-less limiting social and civil life of man: this concrete fabric naturally provided him with his essential means of

---

[7] Cited by T.J. Reed, *Thomas Mann: The Uses of Tradition*, London, 1974, 160 (from the *Der Tod in Venedig* notes in the Thomas Mann Archive, Zurich).

representation. But, as we shall see, it was not the source either of the individual and mysterious things he felt driven to express, or of the life-long force that drove him to express. For it is in the unconscious that the creative urge originates; it is our timeless domain, our domain without history; and there we are the citizens of no country. Fantasy holds a special place among the languages in which the unconscious presents itself to consciousness, for it is a language of particular importance to those individuals in whom we celebrate the creative imagination. James's fiction and letters and working notebooks tell us a great deal about this aspect of his life. But however copious and varied it may have been, Henry James's unconscious fantasy — the fantasy that supported and directed his creativeness — was centred on an imaginary body. That is why we must learn to see him as a fantastic anatomist.

2

Preliminary Investigation

> I look back with wonder and pity to the wretchedly bad basis I have always been on.
>
> Henry, letter to William, October 1887

Henry James laboured to prove himself a great novelist. For all that he may have teased his readers with the bait of a "Figure in [his] Carpet", he espoused a consistent ideal of privacy and there is no reason to suppose that he wished to leave posterity any private communication, still less a meticulous guide to his unconscious mind. And yet, in an obscure corner of his work — "Theodolinde", an unlikely tale of 1878, the year of William James's marriage — that is what we find. Granted the "guide" masquerades as a farcical short story, a story as strained and eccentric as its author's desire for concealment or repudiation could contrive. And yet there it is, creaking and unsung, harbouring more secrets than its more celebrated brothers. Naturally, it is the tale of a body. But that body is not simply the hairdresser's window-dummy with whom the central character, Sanguinetti, falls in love. It is true that she supplies an indispensable central image. Yet she is in the text as a clue, not a solution. She is a signpost and a witticism. The question is where she is directing our gaze and at whose expense the joke is delivered. We can best imagine her as a bright anatomical plate around which an elaborate but faded explanatory and classificatory apparatus is assembled. Evidently we must learn to read in the margins of her story.

Like much of James's work, "Theodolinde" is, in its way, a tale about marriage. When the hero's unlikely purchase is installed at his home, it is the figure of an extraordinary marriage that stares out at us. Now this lover of a window-doll has in common with a number of James's fictional men that his sexuality seems precisely arranged for comic depreciation. But in this story the familiar amused and ironic narrative manner that we find in other tales is pushed over the border of urbane jest into downright facetiousness. Elsewhere, it is James himself who tells us that "no state of mind is as frolicsome as great distress",[1] and it is a lesson to illuminate the sportive extravagances of this tale whose roots are fixed in deep anxieties. But the facetious does not exhaust its armoury of evasiveness. For this early tale shapes itself into a paradoxical form that will continue to be deeply characteristic of James's work: the confessional narrative that constantly displaces and thereby conceals its own centre. In twenty years *The Turn of the Screw* will supply the supreme example of the type. There the unnamed narrative "I" passes an obscure contagion to "poor Douglas" who, in his turn, bequeaths it to the Master of Bly and to Peter Quint. All the tale's men exchange guilty looks, to say nothing of the "little gentleman". This multiple displacement of centre is found in a more embryonic form in "Theodolinde", where the floridly painted central character serves partly as a screen for the narrator. We would see more clearly that the narrator is the real centre of interest had he not created this extravagant diversion. With the beguiling freedom of secrecy, the tale's host paints himself in the portrait of Sanguinetti, who "in spite of his very foreign name ... was a genuine compatriot of my own".[2] We must try to determine what relationship links these partial portraits.

As if to fix in him indelibly the sign of comedy, Sanguinetti is made diminutive in name. In fact, his name, once announced, is made the key-signature of the characterization that is to follow. Diminutives are made to multiply around him. So, within a few pages, he is a "little man", a "little bachelor", a "little model", a

---

[1] *The Tales of Henry James*, ed. M. Aziz, 3 vols, Oxford, 1973- , I, 256.

[2] *Tales*, III, 143.

"little gentleman" who (as a collector) makes "little purchases". When the narrator falls to imaginary matchmaking, we are scarcely surprised to learn his opinion that Sanguinetti's ideal partner would be a "little woman".[3] It would be a mistake, however, to assume that what we are dealing with here is a condescension merely sportive — and one more or less justified by the amorous absurdities towards which Sanguinetti is propelling himself. For the insistently diminishing irony takes a wilfully — but by no means impertinently — *anatomical* form: for example, the tale does indeed — quite literally, in the display-doll — come up with a "little woman" for Sanguinetti. But it is worth noting that the narrator's unremitting habit of diminution is not exercised exclusively on Sanguinetti. The diminutiveness attributed to the misguided lover fails to confine itself there. There is an insidious verbal and conceptual seepage of the idea beyond the contours of the central character. For the imagery of littleness becomes reflexive and begins to intrude, unbidden, on our very knowing and "superior" narrator. This turns out to be of no small importance.

He, as the story opens, is standing on his little balcony waiting for his — we are assured — eccentric guest. The splendours of Paris stretch beneath him as he embarks on the tragi-comic history of Sanguinetti. But if the tale of Sanguinetti is to be the story of a diminished or inadequate body, the fictional shadow of a ruined sexuality, it is by no means with with an evocation of sensual impoverishment that he begins. Indeed, "Theodolinde" opens with a veritable orgy of sensations, with the narrator's overwhelmingly rich and jubilant celebration of his senses, which are stimulated to ecstacy by the sights and tastes and smells of the great city. If we expected spare and tallow forms we meet instead the God of Excess. And of False Wayfaring. For here is a devious and calculated opening. It is as though the story must begin boastfully before its *descent* to Sanguinetti, as though our narrator is intent that we should suppose ourselves to be touching the pulse of true vitality before he turns to anatomize a man who has lost his way.

---

[3] *Ibid.*, 141-49 *passim*.

But although the narrator's impressions are strong and insistent, they cannot vanquish our own sense of relative and differential values. For one thing, he never leaves his perch. And what he takes in from his balcony is not even a multitudinous array of what the great city offers so much as, principally, a narrow band of the *visible* — its narrowness determined by the bias of his own imagination. So he fixes above all, out of the whole scene, on the hairdressing shop and notes there the gentlemen who have had "their whiskers trimmed"; he remarks too the "detached human tresses" that adorn the window; and when he sees his guest loitering there, he wonders whether Sanguinetti intends to buy a "solitary pendent curl" for a postulated object of his affections. When the narrator's gaze fixes next on the restaurant, it is to examine a lady begin to eat her soup "with her little finger very much curled out".[4] These observations, then, — promoted to images in the story — are as insistent and as single in character as the diminutives used of Sanguinetti. Indeed, it is important to realize that they too are diminutive in character, but add the notion of the actual or imminent detachment of what is small from a larger mass on which it is merely an excrescence. The perverse selectiveness of these observations is difficult to ignore and it gives them the character of an involuntary disclosure. It is the narrator's unconscious that speaks in these details and it is difficult to escape the conclusion that the affirmed sensory "wealth" of his experience is tinged with a very distinct shade of anxiety.

Which brings us back to the general riot of the senses out of which these particular images detach themselves. In a story that quite explicitly concerns itself — in Sanguinetti — with a diminished man and his tastes, we may be forgiven for insisting on the spatial or postural relation of things. To recapitulate: the would-be joyous narrator of the opening sequence of "Theodolinde" is not on the Parisian streets but perched high above them on a balcony. His situation is perfectly in keeping with his general pretence of looking down on Sanguinetti. Moreover, his orgy involves only those senses which have their anatomical seat in the head. For him, the whole range of human

---

[4] *Ibid.*, 139-40.

experience has shrunken to what can be seen or smelt or tasted: the restaurant tables glittering with glass and silver, the aroma of a chocolate shop whose wares he delights in, the rich exhalation of a restaurant, the curious smells that drift up from the hairdresser's shop. Now the balcony or elevated perch is a recurrent motif in James's work. We will find it late in *The Ambassadors* just as we may find it early in the autobiographical *Notes of a Son and Brother*, where, as an ailing twelve year old, Henry James hangs over the Parisian scene with the odd feeling that he already "possessed mentally"[5] all that lay below. Jamesian balconies have a regularly dual significance: for while their elevation confers an obvious advantage or privilege, that same fact defines a limitation. In "Theodolinde" the narrator's high perch cannot be taken as a mere neutral architectural fact, shorn of significance. For James has given it a precise, if unconscious, anatomical import: it formulates the bias of the narrator's experience towards the head, marks the literal elevation of his senses above the visceral. We should have no doubt that this is an impoverishment, however it may masquerade as its opposite.[6]

So it is that the distance separating the narrator from Sanguinetti is rather smaller — and their kinship rather closer — than he would have us believe. Indeed, in the history of Sanguinetti, the narrator, and the window-doll, we have the fictional elaboration of a few closely-related unconscious ideas. For we must remind ourselves that these images and situations are part of the naturally-unified psychic manufacture of Henry James, albeit the socialized and licensed phychical stuff that we call fiction. It will constitute our principal mode of access to his unconscious mind.

We are only at the beginning of our investigation, but it is perhaps legitimate to ask ourselves what tentative preliminary conclusions about its creator may be drawn from this story in

---

[5] *Henry James: Autobiography*, ed. F.W. Dupee, London, 1956, 159.

[6] For a consideration of the unconscious mechanism of representation by opposites, see chapter 6(A) ("The Work of Condensation") of Freud's *The Interpretation of Dreams*, in *The Complete Psychological Works of Sigmund Freud*, IV-V.

whose centre reigns an artificial and incomplete female body, this cerebral story from which much of the life of the body is excluded. At the heart of the piece is the narrator's depreciation of his "little" compatriot. In this he appears to externalize and thereby repudiate qualities which are also his own. His attitude of rivalry is mostly hidden in a knowingness and superiority that is not well grounded. For neither in him nor indeed elsewhere does the story provide us with the image of a more convincing and determined masculinity. But rather than a conscious avowal of lack, we are treated to a tactic of anatomical displacement. That is, the unconscious images of a troubled masculinity that find covert representation in both the narrator and Sanguinetti seem to involve libido that has been displaced upwards and exchanged for the various modes of "higher" sensory experience. This upward migration of libido has not failed to achieve a specious positive. We have seen the narrator's boastfulness; and indeed his upper realm constitutes such a jealously hermetic and self-sufficient world that it displays a creative synaesthesia. So, for example, the taste of what is remote can be synthesized out of the other senses. The emanations of the restaurant are pronounced "succulent" and the radiance of the hairdresser's cosmetic bottles is "appetizing".[7] However, none of this polymorphous freedom can disguise the simple fact that the lower — genital — body is missing. So, correspondingly, in the female sphere, the dummy, the "little woman" exists "only from the waist upward", graciously reciprocating the fate of the tale's men.[8] All of which means that when Sanguinetti is presented in terms of what is little, the epithet is, in fact, secretly alluding to an imaginary male body that is not so much diminished as incomplete. It too is a body that ceases at the waist, but that is incomplete because it is damaged or has lost something. For as we have noted, the images of diminution in the story are consistently associated with images of physical detachment which, as we now see, actually *explain* them. What is little is what may easily be lost. This amounts to saying that "Theodolinde" appears to have its psychic basis in an anatomically

---

[7] *Tales*, III, 138, 141.

[8] Ibid.,153.

representable anxiety and strongly suggests the presence of such an anxiety in the unconscious fantasy of Henry James. It is, in addition, an anxiety evidently related to a position of rivalry with another man.

In 1913, exactly half a lifetime after "Theodolinde", Henry James, lately autobiographer, set down his account of a dream for which we have no date. He called it a nightmare — "the most admirable nightmare of my life" — and there are good reasons for looking on it as the dream of his life, the distillation into a fantastic inner scenario of the main psychic elements of his earthly existence. In the dream, he had been first a sleeper, then a sleeper starting up suddenly to defend himself against a would-be intruder pressing hard on his locked door. But this "agent, creature or presence" is suddenly routed by the dreamer, and flies for his life down a "tremendous, glorious hall" that James identifies as the Galerie d'Apollon of the Louvre:

> The climax of this extraordinary adventure — which stands alone for me as a dream-adventure founded in the deepest, quickest, clearest act of cogitation and comparison, act indeed of life-saving energy, as well as in unutterable fear — was the sudden pursuit, through an open door, along a huge high saloon, of a just dimly-descried figure that retreated in terror before my rush and dash (a glare of inspired reaction from irresistible but shameful dread,) out of the room I had a moment before been desperately, and all the more abjectly, defending by the push of my shoulder against hard pressure on lock and bar from the other side. The lucidity, not to say the sublimity, of the crisis had consisted of the great thought that I, in my appalled state, was probably still more appalling than the awful agent, creature or presence, whatever he was, whom I had guessed, in the suddenest wild start from sleep, the sleep within my sleep, to be making for my place of rest. The triumph of my impulse, perceived in a flash as I acted on it by myself at a bound, forcing the door outward, was the grand thing, but the great point of the whole was the wonder of my final recognition. Routed, dismayed, the tables turned upon him by my so surpassing him for straight aggression and dire intention, my visitant was already but a diminished spot in the long perspective, the tremendous, glorious hall, as I say, over the far-gleaming floor of which, cleared for the occassion of its great

line of priceless vitrines down the middle, he sped for *his* life, while a great storm of thunder and lightning played through the deep embrasures of high windows at the right. The lightning that revealed the retreat revealed also the wonderous place and, by the same amazing play, my young imaginative life in it of long before, the sense of which, deep within me, had kept it whole, preserved it to this thrilling use; for what in the world were the deep embrassures and the so polished floor but those of the Galerie d'Apollon of my childhood?[9]

For the moment, we must set aside the extraordinary thing that the ageing novelist's language had become and consider first of all the physical setting of the dream. It is well-known that the artistic splendours of the Louvre were early associated for Henry James with the military triumphs of Napoleon I. If the Galerie d' Apollon in Napoleon's Louvre was for the young visitor of 1855 a "bridge over to style", it was a style (as Edel points out) punningly associated with the name Napoleon itself.[10] It is also worth recalling that, in his final delirium (1916), the ancient novelist took on the identity of the great soldier of whom he had read so much, and dictated in his name a letter to his dead brother and sister, organizing the redecoration of the Louvre:

> I call your attention to the previous enclosed transcripts of plans and designs for the decoration of certain apartments of the palaces, here, of the Louvre and the Tuileries, which you will find addressed in detail to artists and workmen who are to take them in hand. I commit them to your earnest care till the questions relating to this important work are fully settled. When that is the case I shall require of you further zeal and further taste. For the present the course is definitely marked out, and I beg you to let me know from stage to stage definitely how the scheme promises and what results it may be held to inspire. It is, you will see, of a great scope, a majesty unsurpassed by any work of the kind yet undertaken in France. Please understand I regard these plans as fully developed and as having had my last consideration and look forward to no patchings nor perversions, and with no question of

---

[9] *Autobiography*, 196-97.

[10] Leon Edel, *The Life of Henry James* (revised edn), 2 vols, Harmondsworth, 1977, I, 60-61.

modifications either economic or aesthetic. This will be the case with all further projects of your affectionate
                                                            Napoleone.[11]

The magnificent exaltation of this is quite clearly delusional, but a deeply-rooted identification gives it an uncanny sureness and an infectious buoyancy. It seems clear that the imaginative veteran of no campaign, who had grown old reading military memoirs, the remnant of the young man whose "obscure hurt"[12] had kept him from the war of 1861, it seems clear that James had long ago found in the Emperor an alternative or ideal self, an embodiment of his ego-ideal.[13] For there was one whose artistic spoils were the fruit of martial prowess, not of a graceless alternative to manhood, or a mere "negative of combat".[14] To Henry James, assuredly, the Galerie d'Apollon was not simply a place among others. It was a place which in all probability had early lost its historical and public character, its externality (it "became for years what I can only term a splendid scene of things"[15]), and had taken on a private and unconscious significance. It is probable that all men have recurrent dream topographies (for they clearly have recurrent dream images), as constant as the outer world's locations, or more constant. In this sense, the Galerie d'Apollon was a familiar and persistent terrain to Henry James and his Louvre dream may be taken to reveal some of the permanent features of his unconscious fantasy.

A familiar but also a *family* terrain: for we may assert with Freud that the fundamental level of signification in dreams is infantile, and that we cannot suppose any dream satisfactorily

---

[11] *Henry James: Letters*, ed. Leon Edel, 4 vols, Cambridge: Mass. and London, 1974-84, IV, 811.

[12] *Autobiography*, 415.

[13] See for example J. Laplanche and J.-B. Pontalis, *The Language of Psychoanalysis*, trans. D. Nicholson-Smith, London, 1988, 144-45.

[14] *Autobiography*, 417.

[15] *Ibid.*, 196.

interpreted till a link has been established with the reconstituted early life of the dreamer. But what is infantile in the elements we have examined so far? A man esteems the man he might have been, in a fantasy of power and success — a wish tolerably adult. We must press further into this "admirable nightmare".

It is interesting that the door that protects the dreamer opens in both directions. Barred against the pushing intruder, it initially threatens to open inwards; but then, the tables turned, the dreamer, "forcing the door outward", pursues his assailant. The importance of this detail is that it provides us with a valuable indication — through imagery — of the dream's symmetrical (and therefore reversible) construction. This is already clear enough in the central situational turning of the tables, but if we hold fast to it as a reigning structural and representational principle, it will enable us to arrive at a fuller re-construction of James's dream. For it is, of course, necessary to assume that the dream is incomplete, both as dreamed (on account of the inveterate and skilful economies of the dream-work[16]) and as reported to us (on account of the repressing and disguising deletions of memory). What expansion or reconstruction helps us to, above all, is a clear view of the nature of the "agent, creature or presence" that begins by threatening the dreamer. In the reported dream we have, in addition to these epithets, the mention of "a just dimly-descried figure that retreated in terror before my rush". We can assert with confidence that the figure would not need to be represented as "dimly-descried" if he had indeed the anonymity of an "agent, creature or presence". This means that the identity of the known attacher is disguised. Disguised too, or at any rate lacking, is any exact account of the threat that he poses to the sleeper, except that he has apparently proposed to strike as he slept. It is at this point that we need to invoke our principle of symmetrical construction (or reversibility) and assume that the thing the dreamer does to his assailant, reveals what the assailant had wished to do to him.

---

[16] See *The Interpretation of Dreams*, especially chapter 6 ("The Dream-work") for detailed elucidation of this and other terms used in this sequence.

But what does the dreamer do to the intruder, apart from forestalling his design and sending him packing? What we struggle with above all here is the fact that the exact dream dreamt by Henry James is in many ways lost. We are condemned to resemble archaeologists as much as interpreters of this dream. Lost, above all, is what we may call the dream's own rhetoric. It is as though we had been asked to assess a lost poem from a new poem worked up out of a few surviving phrases by a master-forger. Clearly, our best chance is to identify these original phrases, the authentic unconscious discourse.

Freud teaches us that all dreams are, in their essential nature, wish-fulfilments and that, in a dream, the fundamental wish is not merely formulated but actually represented as fulfilled. The point at which the wish is fulfilled may be taken as the dynamic centre of the dream. It seems to me that the heart of James's Louvre dream is not the comparatively vague defeat of the intruder but precisely his *spatial diminution*:

> my visitant was already but a diminished spot in the long perspective.

The wish hereby fulfilled may be taken to reverse a feared outcome that, as we formulate it, helps us to define an important element in assailant's imagined enterprise: he wished to make the dreamer tiny, to tower over him in sleep, to make *him* "a spot in the long perspective". The dream thus rehearses a childhood terror and fabricates a jubilant solution in which a dreaded outcome is both averted and inverted. An infantile fantasy of (Napoleonic) omnipotence vanquishes an infantile fantasy of annihilation.

As one whose adult trade was to be in words, Henry James did not have an easy relationship with what must have been among his first of these. As late as 1882, (the year in which his father died), he was still suffering irritation at the public blurring of identities that resulted from his sharing the name "Henry" with his father. (William at least shared his name with an ancestor who had had the good grace to die long before.) It seems clear that, from earliest days, Henry had felt his identity threatened by this irrepressible family tradition, and he more than once protested against it. In vain: for another Alice and another Henry waited in the wings. Practically, he adopted the "junior" subscript to his signature while his father lived, and he felt sufficiently diminished by this to sign his name only with an initial "H" until he could discard the "Jnr" and become "Henry James" entire.

Interestingly, in Henry's depreciating remarks on this topic, the "junior" took on a quasi-anatomical status as "that appendage" — as transferred an epithet as ever was. It is interesting too (as Edel notes) that, with the passage of years, the pen that was destined for 40 years to sign "junior", blurred and eroded these few letters until nothing remained of them but a diminished spot.[17]

The psychoanalytic point-of-view once granted, it is neither surprising nor original to affirm of Henry James (or of any other truly imaginative writer) that his early psychic history is symbolically inscribed in the situations and characters of the fiction that he elaborates out of it. But there is something else here that needs to be grasped. In this future writer, family conflict — and whatever instinctual conflict may have determined or come into association with it — assumed very early a verbal character. This means that James's peculiar adult investment in specifically verbal manufacture — he becomes a novelist, not a sculptor — is from the beginning *itself* already heavily laden with meaning over and above whatever he choses to say with his words. In a developmental sense, we should not take James's late style for granted. It cannot be without significance that the child from whom a single word seemed originally to withhold full identity, embarked on a career of asserting that undiminished identity in words that constitute perhaps the most extravagant and elaborate verbal signature in human history.

It is my belief that the psychological investigation of an artist cannot properly take the medium of his endeavours as a given, and address itself — in all naiveté — to matters of "content" only. Evidently, Henry James's adult creative medium was words. Accordingly, a central task of this study will be to reach as full an understanding as possible of what will emerge as James's

---

[17] *Life*, I, 50-51.

pathological relation to language, a relation originating in infancy. (I believe that such a pathological relation to words may be osberved in many creative writers.) This need involve no unconscionable narrowing of our field of interest. For, properly understood, James's unconscious relation to language already embodies those same unconscious ideas and impulses that, in a real sense, find only supplementary representation in his fictions. But since this relation is woven into the whole fabric of his living and of his creativeness, it is an intricate one and we cannot hope to unravel all its threads at once. To speak more technically: James's relation to language is overdetermined.[18] At this juncture I am conscious of having addressed only the self-affirmative side of that relation — a grandiose self-affirmation mustered to rout primitive threats and anxieties that thus far both a tale and a dream have set before us.

Not indeed that the fears of being a son and a brother included no anatomical component for Henry James's imagination. His father's missing leg was doubtless a vivid daily testimony to the possibility of serious mutilation. We can measure the impression made on the child from the adult's fiction. A figure who has lost a leg limps into the house of fiction with James's first published story ("A Tragedy of Error") in 1864. He appears to install himself for a long stay: forty four years later, in "The Jolly Corner" (1908), he is still there. (Later still, a "limp" will find its way into the deranged deathbed dictations.[19]) In all cases, he is the enemy, the one to be overcome, and he proves a formidable adversary. And this ghostly figure is not merely there in person at the beginning and at the end of the son's artistic career. He reigns throughout in secret as the liability to sickness or injury of the imaginary men who spring up to people Henry's fiction. (For the child's view of what has happened to others, helps create his ideas of what may happen to him.) And invariably, it is to the idea of anatomical loss that Henry turns for the expression of extreme emotion: the death of William "has cut

---

[18] *The Language of Psychoanalysis*, 292-93.

[19] *Letters*, IV, 810.

into me deep down, even as an absolute mutilation"; when he stands before his childhood house in the bleak new century, he feels "amputated of half my history".[20] There seems little doubt that an anxiety permanently attached to images of physical mutilation occupied an important place in James's unconscious life. Now if this anxiety fixed itself on words (and was, in addition, to seek a verbal release) that was because his father's taking away of the word that was his, seemed to justify a fear of loss or injury that was already established. We may surmise that for Henry all the urgency of palpable physical fear pressed on the verbal arena and abolished for ever the possibility of a conflict-free relation to language. That is why the direct and voluble William James's exasperation with his younger brother's late style is so telling: "Say it *out*, for God's sake ...."[21] It is Henry's early anxieties over words that supply the prehistory of William's impatience. When William is dead and silent, Henry's autobiography of 1913 ("an attempt to place together some particulars of the early life of William James"[22]) will cover him in a vast and extraordinary mausoleum of words.

But words are so evidently and predictably the medium of literary activity that we must struggle to reach a fuller understanding of the almost occult or talismanic value that they had for Henry James. A fragment of family history comes to our aid. In the summer of 1913, William's daughter, Peggy, crossed the ocean to visit her remarkable uncle. One day she fell to ventriloquizing her dead father (who, on the publication of *The American Scene* in 1907 had pleaded with his erring younger brother to revert to his "older director manner"[23]) and rebuked her uncle for the loss of strength and simplicity of expression in his work. She received this remarkable reply:

---

[20] *Life*, II, 725, 598.

[21] *The Letters of William James*, II, 278.

[22] *Autobiography*, 3.

[23] *The Letters of William James*, II, 278.

"I hate the American simplicity. I glory in the piling up of complications of every sort. If I could pronounce the name James in any different and more elaborate way I should be in favour of doing it."[24]

It is striking that a defence of the style provoked by so threatening a family questioner as William's daughter, turns immediately for illustration to the saying of names, those early representatives of his anxiety. We can measure the perceived threat by the near-grandiosity summoned to rout it. And as a disclosure of what supports James's syntactic oddity, we can take what he says almost literally. The syntax *is* a symbolic and boastful elaboration of a name that threatened to hide the one who bore it — unlike William's name, which was his own. But this by no means exhausts our tentative psychopathology of James's use of words. William's complaint is now a familiar critical observation — namely, that in the late stage of his development (say, after 1897), James's sentences became by degrees so minutely subordinated and elaborate that, in the end, he arrived almost at a private language. But however he may before Peggy have insisted on what was controlled and deliberate in his complications, we catch in this family anecdote more the note of the childish and the wilful. In the extravagance of his self-affirmation there is assuredly something unsettling, more than a hint (for all the implied deliberateness) of something out of control. In the investigation of psychopathological conditions, the circumstances of onset are generally of great interest. Let us follow the same principle here.

In 1897, right on the threshold of the late style, James's work habits suffered a significant change. He began to dictate aloud where before he had simply written. This remedy for a muscular cramp proved so deeply congenial that he used it for the rest of his days. It is well know that James's manner of speech had always been a little odd: in 1882, Edmund Gosse noted its "punctilious hesitancy"; Max Beerbohm made James "the greatest of hesitators"; while, to Edith Wharton, his "slow way of speech was really the partial victory over a stammer which in his

---

[24] *Life*, II, 763.

boyhood had been though incurable".²⁵ We cannot understand the fuller import of James's remarks to William's daughter unless we notice that, whereas her query related to writing, James's retort insisted on speech. I believe that dictation became to James not merely a mode of work but a peculiar kind of peasurable indulgence. The slowness and endless deferrals that are the essential being of the resultant syntax had as their more immediate purpose a long physical savouring of the act of articulation. I speak of unconscious purpose, for this pleasure in dictation (with its "help to do over and over"²⁶) is not to be mistaken for the pleasure that any wordsmith might take in the practice of his art. It is closer to the pleasure that a child finds in his realized capacity to create a sound. An this analogy, together with that of physical savouring, does not invoke idle comparisons.

For the crown of the era of dictation was James's adoption of "Fletcherism", around 1904. Horace Fletcher was an American food faddist, author of *The New Glutton and Epicure*, who advocated that food should be chewed into liquidity before swallowing. "The divine Fletcher"²⁷ provided James with this strange late enthusiasm, and in 1906 he pronounced himself a fanatic. (Franz Kafka succumbed around the same time.²⁸) Fletcher was even to be on one occasion a table guest at Lamb House, and Burgess Noakes's bemused memoir tells us how "he and Mr James sat munching each bit of beef sixty times".²⁹ But, in general, the habit of Fletcherizing made James reluctant to eat with others, since, clearly, the more social habit involved speech,

---

[25] H. Montgomery Hyde, *Henry James at Home*, London, 1969, 17, 203; Edith Wharton, *A Backward Glance*, 177-78.

[26] *Letters*, IV, 247.

[27] *Ibid.*, 374.

[28] See, for example, Ronald Hayman, *K: A Biography of Kafka*, London, 1981, 248; Ernst Pawel, *The Nightmare of Reason: A Life of Franz Kafka*, London, 1984, 208-09.

[29] *Henry James at Home*, 138.

for which this protracted mastication had become an alluring equivalent. The ideal was a cosy, wordless, ungregarious feeding in which the habit could be pushed to its limit without interruptions or concessions to adult presence. So deep a pleasure is not indulged without a guilty ambivalence, and by 1909 James is seeking reassurance as to the value of the method.[30] By February 1910 an episode of depression has laid him very low and a letter to William makes Fletcherism the source of all his woes.[31] Yet when an alarmed (and himself ailing) William dispatched his son across a wintry Atlantic, young Harry found his uncle "secretly Fletcherizing" again, feeling that he had "got hold of something"[32].

Psychological processes often become clearer in their more extreme manifestations. It seems that what we are dealing with here is a profoundly regressive personality — a personality regressing, precisely, to the oral levels of infantile libidinal organisation. It is thus an involuntary literalism that makes James confess of the liquid pleasures of Fletcherism that they have "renewed the sources of my life".[33] For it is — among other things — an object-free autoerotic orality that has declared its presence in James's extraordinary late investment in words. And this vividly pathological development helps us to understand the stealthier psychic processes of the earlier fiction. Of "Theodolinde", for example. For what we are now in a position to see, is that the tale's emphasis on the higher, non-genital body is not simply a representationally convenient upward displacement of libido but, in essence, a defensive migration of libido to an earlier — secretly unabandoned — stage of development. The oral-gustatory and olfactory components of infantile sexuality are what provide the invisible source of the balcony observer's orgy of sensations; so

---

[30] *Letters*, IV, 516.

[31] Ibid., 546-58.

[32] *Life*, II, 718.

[33] *Letters*, IV, 374.

too the "polymorphous"[34] plasticity of this stage of erotic organisation underlies the accomplished synaesthesia he enjoys. And there is no contradiction in James's arriving at a sophisticated verbal transcription of infantile modes of experience. For, as we have seen, in James's late pathological development, infantile pleasure is not merely described in words: words themselves regressively reconstitute the oral component of that pleasure. For Henry James, dictation rested on unconscious anatomical fantasy.

We must not lose sight of the dream from which we also set out. It seems to me likely that the Louvre dream should be understood as dramatizing and then wishfully reversing a castration anxiety. It was this same anxiety — the various manifestations of which we have been considering — that drove Henry James down the path of regression to pre-Oedipal organizations of the libido.[35] There words — in flight from the signs of diminution or lack that attach to them in the conflicts of the Oedipal phase — re-enter the oral phase which factitiously makes them the signs of phallic integrity and affirmation. The act of speech, the act of dictation is made to affirm individual wholeness. In this we have in essence the grandiose triumph of the Louvre dream with its vanquished would-be assailant. And this also means that it would be a mistake to dismiss the dream's grandiose solution to the fear of annihilation as a wishful fantasy merely. For the self-affirmation visible in the dream had found concrete and waking expression also. We can make the same point in a different way. The infantile material we have been reviewing has inevitably a dual character. In common with all psychoneurotic processes, James's regressiveness may have marked a flight from the turbulent loving and hating, the hoping and fearing and, above all, the rivalries of close human relating; but it was, simultaneously, a movement towards a position of greater strength and security. That safer terrain we can now designate as

---

[34] For an elaboration of this and other associated concepts used in the following discussion, see *Three Essays on the Theory of Sexuality* in *The Complete Psychological Works of Sigmund Freud*, VII, 123-245.

[35] *The Language of Psychoanalysis*, 56-59; 386-88; 328-29; 236-40.

that of verbal potency. And without the fearsome anxiety that roused him to a project of verbal self-affirmation, his words would have belonged, like yours or mine, to the lexicon only. They live with their special life because they are part of the very substance of an unconscious drama.

In its fashion, James's account of the Louvre dream — with its maddening syntactic extravagance — says and resays all of this. We laid our earlier emphasis on the jubilant triumph of the dreamer and his diminution of the assailant to "a mere spot in the long perspective". But, in that long perspective, the attendant lightning discovers a "wondrous place". And it is precisely *by* the "wondrous place" and its perspective that the intruder is diminished. We may assert with some confidence that the grand, glorious and majestic place of the dream had come to represent the novelist's creative self. It was, if one will, his unconscious hall of fiction, reserved for a jubilant affirmation of self. But it rested on the painful foundation that the dream discloses: the intruder may only reach the dreamer (secure within the palace of words that is his remade self) by passing along the same halls, lined with awesome images of decapitation,[36] that the dreamer himself once braved — the only path to his "place of rest".

There are, of course, as I have hinted, other determinants of James's language-pathology; but these must await our consideration of *The Turn of the Screw* in a later chapter. Of more immediate concern is the fact that there are also other important features of his orality than those which I have indicated thus far. In an important early refinement of Freud's theory of libidinal development, Karl Abraham distinguished between an earlier and a later oral phase — the earlier dominated by the pleasurable activity of sucking, but the later (oral-sadistic phase) by biting and devouring.[37] The later phase differs crucially from the earlier in implying an ambivalent relation to objects (persons), against

---

[36] *Autobiography*, 194-95.

[37] Karl Abraham, "A Short View of the Development of the Libido, viewed in the Light of Mental Disorders"(1924), in *Selected Papers of Karl Abraham M.D.*, London, 1927, 408-501.

whom for the first time, — as if in a constituting moment of the properly human — libidinal *and* aggressive impulses, feeling of love and hate, are directed. I believe that we can detect a regression to this phase in Henry's ambivalence over and eventual secretiveness about his "Fletcherizing". In hiding it from the young transatlantic emissary in February of 1910, he was in essence guiltily hiding it from his brother William, himself increasingly ill and indeed in the last months of his life. Moreover, this secret chewing alternated with bouts of "sickishly *loathing* food",[38] a conjunction strongly suggestive of an attempt to escape from oral-sadistic impulses and the unconscious fantasies allied to them. If we add to this — more comprehensively — that Henry suffered episodes of depressive illness as William's health declined and immediately after his death, it is hard to escape the suspicion that Henry's ambivalence about Fletcherism stood for his ambivalence over oral sadistic trends in his own make-up of which William was now the object. (A contamination of the verbal sphere by such oral-sadistic fantasies will be central to our reading of *The Turn of The Screw*.) It seems that unconscious phantasies of harming William were revitalized by his physical decline and now found expression in the shameful but secretly pleasurable Fletcherism — the oral modality doubtless phase-appropriate to a childhood conflict and already providing a fixation point.[39] This means that the episodic "food loathing" depressions that preceded and followed William's death involved an intermittent directing against the self of the oral sadistic impulses for which chewing had provided an alluring expression. If we follow Abraham, we can further add that the more "innocent", pre-ambivalent oral-gustatory level of organisation is also sought as an escape from the oral-sadistic. Again this accords with our findings in "Theodolinde". I remarked at the outset that this revealing story was written in 1878, the year of William's marriage. We must now press further into this important circumstance.

---

[38] *Letters*, IV, 547.

[39] *The Language of Psychoanalysis*, 162-65.

For the tale was not simply contemporary with the marriage of Henry's elder brother but was in essentials an unconscious, imaginative reaction to it. The contest of the nameless narrator and Sanguinetti — the "little-blooded" fellow — is a disguised tale of sibling rivalry.[40] The higher and superior — the elder figure — was in reality William, as Henry was the little brother who felt he would never make up the fifteen months that separated them. In the tale, this situation is wishfully reversed — or rather, a reversal is attempted. But the depreciating and diminishing qualities that the narrator externalizes onto Sanguinetti contaminate his own higher position: he cannot escape from them, for they are his own.[41] Moreover, as we have seen, even his specious triumph is bought in a dubious currency, involving as it does a regressive mustering of forces from pre-Oedipal levels with their more primitive modes of relation to objects.

Clearly these conclusions have been arrived at in large part by a careful psychoanalytically-oriented reading of "Theodolinde". But there are other directions in which we can turn for indications of Henry's attitude to William's married state. To his notebooks, for example. These provide the closest approach to the clinical method of free-association that is available to us, for

---

[40] At a meeting of the Northern Irish Guest Study Group of the International Psychoanalytic Association in January 1993, the psychoanalyst Dr Malcolm Pines made the interesting suggestion that a punning relation to the French words "sans Guillaume" may have contributed to the name Sanguinetti.

[41] An interesting glimpse of Henry's unconscious tendency to depreciate or belittle William is provided in Henry's notebook entry for 23 May 1901, where he records a new idea for a story about a husband who is "so overwhelming and inconsiderate a chatterbox" that he fails to discover the concealed "gift" for talk of his wife (feminine counterpart), this having been kept down, kept in abeyance in her connection with him. What makes Henry's idea so interesting is that the William Jameses had been staying with him in Sussex while William prepared his Gifford Lectures (*The Varieties of Religious Experience*) for delivery in Edinburgh from June 1901. See *The Complete Notebooks of Henry James*, eds Leon Edel and Lyall H. Powers, New York, 1987, 194-95.

here Henry set down, more or less at random, ideas and situations that occurred to him as germs from which stories might grow. In this dense mass of material it is naturally given to some imagined situations to occur more than once. But there is one repetition that in the present connection is supremely worthy of our attention. This is an idea that is recorded in the notebooks on 11 September 1900 and then again on 21 April 1911. It was destined never to be worked up into a story:

> Alice [William's wife] related a day or two ago another little anecdote, of New England, of "Weymouth" origin, in which there might be some small very good thing. Some woman of that countryside — some woman and her husband — were waked at night by a sound below-stairs which they knew, or believed, must be burglars, and it was a question of the husband's naturally going down to see. But the husband declined — wouldn't stir, said he wasn't armed, hung back, etc., and his wife declared that in that case she must. But her disgust and scorn. "You mean to say you'll let me?" "Well, I can't prevent you. But I won't — !" She goes down, leaving him, and in the lower regions finds a man — a young man of the place — whom she knows. He's not a professional housebreaker, naturally, only a fellow in bad ways, in trouble, wanting to get hold of some particular thing, to sell, realise it, that they have. Taken in the act, and by her, his assurance fails him, while hers rises, and her view of the situation. He too is a poorish creature — he makes no stand. She threatens to denounce him (he keeps her from calling) and he pleads with her not to ruin him. The little scene takes place between, and she consents at last, this first time, to let him off. But if ever again — why, she'll this: which counts all the more against him — so, look out! He does look out, she lets him off and out, he escapes, and she returns to her husband. He has heard the voices below, making out, however, nothing, and he knows something has taken place. She admits part of it — says there was somebody, and she has let him off. Who was it them? — he is all eagerness to know. Ah, but this she won't tell him, and she meets curiosity with derision and scorn. She will never tell him; he won't be able to find out; and he will never know — so that he will be properly punished for his cowardice.[42]

---

[42] *Ibid.*, 193.

It is the same story that is recorded again at greater length and with some additional elaborations in 1911.[43] (James himself notes the repetition.) The core of the thing seems to me to be the wife's newly-discovered scorn for her prostrated husband upstairs and her secret affiliation with the young intruder down below. We may very reasonably ask ourselves why James repeated the material at all, since in the second and longer version he confesses to feeling that the situation is (artistically speaking) unworkable and can lead nowhere — as indeed it did. The answer is presumably that in April 1911 the pressure of unconscious ideation forced the situation back into consciousness. If we ask how that came about, we meet an intriguing fact.

At the date of both entries — 11 years apart — Henry was sleeping under the same roof as Alice, with William absent. For 11 September 1900 was "the eve of [Alice's] leaving for the U.S., with W[illiam] at Nauheim."[44] That is, Alice was staying with Henry at Lamb House while William had gone (this time alone) to the Bad Nauheim Spa in Germany. At the date of the later entry, 21 April 1911, Henry was staying with Alice at his now deceased brother's Irving Street house in Cambridge, Massachusetts — the former home of his mother and father. (He commuted in these months between Irving Street and New York, being treated psychologically by James Jackson Putnam and Joseph Collins, respectively.) It was this precise family situation — together with the enhanced introspection that accompanied his depressive illness and its treatment — which caused the resurgence of the story into his consciousness. This helps us to identify its likely unconscious significance. For here, as in the story of Sanguinetti, is a tale of two men, a higher and a lower, the higher prostrate and inefficacious, the lower scarcely heroic yet (in the later version) wronged and daring, seeking redress. The younger man is evidently more at home in the lower regions than the "unarmed" upper man, for in these regions he forges an intimacy with the wife, for whom the upstairs man is now unmasked as a coward. In a sense, therefore, the intruder turns the tables on the

---

[43] *Ibid.*, 204-08.

[44] *Ibid.*, 192.

husband and replaces him. The intruder thus contrives the sort of triumph that *mutatis mutandis* is at the heart of the Louvre dream.

Such, then, is the fantasy that Henry James, ancient bachelor, sleeping in the home of his dead parents, now alone with the wife of his dead brother, conjures out of the countless shadows that might assail him. This is as clear an Oedipal fantasy as one could hope to find and what it tells us is that for Henry his brother's marriage re-enacted an Oedipal conflict. In the story the father-brother is dislodged from his (undeserved) nocturnal position alongside the mother-wife. Since Henry Senior had an artificial leg, it is tempting to speculate that a vengeful childish curiosity as to whether father had anything (was "armed") "downstairs" also entered into the fantasy. Viewed in this Oedipal light, the 1911 modifications of the story of 1900 are interesting. For in the second version the story does not end with the intruder's displacement of the husband but rather with his eventual siding with the husband against his (he feels) gratuitously-punishing wife. In other words, now that William is dead, the will to ascendancy finds itself puzzled and checked by a natural movement toward reparation.[45] Small wonder that Henry felt the story could lead to nothing, for the new balance of aggressive and loving tendencies had modified its unconscious purpose.

A few months before the year (1911) was out, Henry James, now back in England, had shaken off the blackness, child of Fletcherism, that had dogged him for almost two years. In January 1912 he wrote to James Jackson Putnam, friend of William and associate of Freud, to announce his improved health and to express his gratitude to the physician who had "tided [him] over three or four bad places during those worst months".[46] The language in which is recovery is announced is most striking, given the issues we have been examining. So he is not merely better but "quite enormously better". The town of Rye he finds too small

---

[45] *The Language of Psychoanalysis*, 388-89.

[46] *Letters*, IV, 597.

now, repairing instead to the "big Babylon" of London as the only place

> adequate for me and worthy, so to speak, of my powers and my infirmities, on the scale of them and proportionate to them .... Speaking in a summary manner I have a *big* enough surface to expand myself nervously upon — and if I had had a bigger one at the time you were seeing me, I probably should have got forward much more continuously.[47]

It is not difficult to turn back from this material to the Louvre dream in which Henry's grandiose triumph involved a making little of his antagonist, who became "a diminished spot in the long perspective". We are now in a position to assess the meaning of this essentially Oedipal contest, though the question of the intruder's identity in the dream is not a simple one. For if he is William he is also Henry Senior and, if him, then also (by reversal) Henry Junior, banished from his intrusion on the primal scene of the parental bed. However this may be, there is no mistaking the jubilant affect in which all these elements are pressed into positive psychic service and no mistaking either the attendant artistic splendours that seem to confirm the dreamer's victory. Appropriately, this artistic dream-place can be met again within James's faction itself. In *The Golden Bowl* (1904), the imagination of wealthy collector, Adam Verver, devises for the people of his native place a "museum of museums, a palace of Art", to redeem them from the "bondage of ugliness":

> Foundations were laid and walls were rising, the structure of the shell all determined; but raw haste was forbidden him in a connexion so intimate with the highest effects of patience and piety; he should belie himself by completing without a touch at least of the majesty of delay a monument to the religion he wished to propagate, the exemplary passion, the passion for perfection at any price. He was far from knowing as yet where he would end ....[48]

---

[47] Ibid., 595-96.

[48] Henry James, *The Golden Bowl*, ed. Gore Vidal, Harmondsworth, 1985, 143.

Adam Verver is of course not quite free from the licenced megalomania of a dreamer, and it is interesting to listen in this passage (and others) to the faint but unmistakable tones of the grandiose Napoleonic letter that we considered earlier. Nor does this exhaust the parallels with the dream, for Adam Verver is a cunning fictional embodiment of the contest of small and great on which the Louvre dream turns. His stupendous wealth means that his fellow mortals treat him as "an infinite agent", a kind of god. Superficially, this attribution is uncomfortable, since nature has framed him "a small spare slightly stale person, deprived of the general prerogative of presence". But although this conqueror of artistic worlds repudiates personal power ("it pressed upon him hard ... this attribution of power"), the reader is not slow to gather that he is possessed of a formidable inner force, albeit that his trick is ceaselessly to indulge the high pleasure of seeming to have none.[49] Spiritual *raffiné*, he has discovered the last luxury of ultimate power in a studied Olympian abstention from using it. So his domination of the novel — as first mover and instigator, and ultimate custodian of all wares and properties — is an exercise in high paradox. He is never apparently other than a "little meditative man" in a straw hat, on the edge of vision, unassuming, inaudible save for his "small perpetual hum of contemplation", and unremarkable but for his "indescribable air of weaving his spell".[50] And yet this nothing is the everything, the Prospero of his Kingdom, the magician to whose tune even princes dance. He is, above all, James's imaginative representative in this most self-conscious of fictions, and it is not difficult to discover the character of the novelist's delighted investment in him. Verver is a fantasy of power and conquest in whom these qualities are disclosed as the secret reserve of personal nullity. But he is also an entirely credible fictional creation — a successful sublimation, for all that he may be a figure unconsciously determined. In James, the unconscious does not assault us in its denuded and unsublimated state. On the whole, his demons do

---

[49] *Ibid.*, 133, 160.

[50] *Ibid.*, 522.

not walk abroad in daylight. (In this respect, in the major fiction, Peter Quint and his female counterpart in *The Turn of the* Screw represent notable exceptions.) Henry James has given us an art founded on neurosis and energized by it. But it is art still, albeit an amost impossible art — the art of minimal sublimation.

3

Case History

> ... turned inside out for the lesson ... it has been given to him to constitute practically — on the demonstrator's table with an attentive circle around — an extraordinary, a magnificent "case".
>
> Henry James, "Gustave Flaubert" (1893)

By the end of his life, the habit of composition had, as we have seen, drawn Henry James into the labyrinth of an extraordinarily individual expression. At least one verbal habit had, however, been with him from the beginning of his writing career. It was an oddity neither of phrasing nor of syntax, but a simple addiction — to the word "case". The habit is clearly detectable from the 1870s, but, forty years on, — by the time we reach the dictated "Prefaces" to the New York Edition — the word is everywhere. It is a mistake, however, to assume (with F.R. Leavis, for example) that James had no clear awareness of his own verbal (and other) idiosyncrasies. "I know that I'm too diffuse when I'm dictating", he confessed to his last secretary, Theodora Bosanquet, — whom he also warned (like her predecessors) of the protracted gaps in his delivery she would have to endure.[1] And to his literary agent, James B. Pinker, he spoke of composing in the way

> I seem condemned to; which is to *overtreat* my subject by developments and amplifications that have, in large part, eventually to be greatly compressed, but to the prior operation

---

[1] Theodora Bosanquet, *Henry James at Work*, London, 1924, 7.

of which the thing owes what is most durable in its quality ....
But you will say that I am "over-treating" this subject too!²

These are general insights, but what of his particular addiction to the word "case"? James *does* appear to have had some awareness of this interesting affliction also, for there is a wonderful comic moment in *The Golden Bowl* when Bob Assingham (who, with his obsessively voyeuristic wife, parodies the agonies and ruminations of the late Jamesian narrative consciousness) breaks out in exasperation at Fanny's choric recitation of the many "cases" that await their obsessive midnight "treatment":

> "Lord, are there so many?"
> "There's Maggie's and the Prince's, and there's the Prince's and Charlotte's."
> "Oh yes; and then," the Colonel scoffed, "there's Charlotte's and the Prince's."
> "There's Maggie's and Charlotte's," she went on — "and there's also Maggie's and mine. I think too that there's Charlotte's and mine. Yes," she mused, "Charlotte's and mine is certainly a case. In short, you see, there are plenty. But I mean," she said, "to keep my head."
> "Are we to settle them all," he enquired, "tonight?"³

But whatever luxuriance of self-mockery the mature artist was able to lay out on his own entrenched habits, the addiction in itself remains unexplained. Why was Henry James so attracted to this little word, and what was the history of his use of it?

One thing that evidently seduced his interest was the word's metaphorical potential. It was an abstract term to be won back to the concrete. So, to the James of the "Prefaces", the artist is an "incorrigible collector of 'cases'", — that is to say, of people and situations that can provoke, sustain and reward artistic interest.⁴ But — as "incorrigible" suggests — an interest in receptacles of (or

---

² *The Letters of Henry James*, ed. Percy Lubbock, 2 vols, London, 1920, I, 15.

³ *The Golden Bowl*, 92.

⁴ *The Art of the Novel: Critical Prefaces*, ed. R. P. Blackmur, New York, 1934, 185.

for) the human spirit is a dangerous thing. Not for nothing is the study of the sinister Dr Austin Sloper full of "things in glass cases". For the artist, like that errant physician, sometimes risks the unprofessional sin of "overtreatment":

> *The Awkward Age* places itself for me ... in a group of small productions exhibiting this perversity, representations of conceived cases in which my process has been to pump the case gaspingly dry, dry not only of superfluous moisture, but absolutely ... of breathable air.[5]

On the other hand, the artist himself can become a "case" — which James makes the just fate of Flaubert:

> Flaubert has been turned inside out for the lesson ... it has been given to him to constitute practically — on the demonstrator's table with an attentive circle around — an extraordinary, a magnificent "case".[6]

The metaphor here is, of course, consciously — and even playfully — exploiting Flaubert's medical upbringing, and the all-too-visible dissections that cast a shadow over his childhood. But we do not need the conspicuous example of Flaubert in order to make a simple observation on all of these typical examples. If it is the general metaphorical promise of the word that supports James's interest in it, there is, nevertheless, a consistent drift of that metaphorical interest in the direction of the medical. This is not to say that all occurrences of the word "case" in James carry a medical meaning, or even a medical innuendo. After all, words do not belong to individuals, nor do individuals independently and arbitrarily determine their meanings. The fact remains, however, that James's long habit of over-using this word has to be understood in relation to his own life — in which it had a private history. Nothing, William James once remarked, "can make a man into a mere lump of egotism" like sickness. What seems to have sustained his brother's life-long fidelity to the word "case",

---

[5] *Ibid.*, 114.

[6] *Henry James: Literary Criticism*, eds Leon Edel and Mark Wilson, 2 vols, New York, 1984, II, 297.

was that, for him, the word itself carried a secret allusion to what he considered his *own* case. On one level, this allusion is to the lumbar and intestinal troubles that, from his early twenties, he referred to *en famille* as his "invalidism". Already in 1870 it is an incorrigible companion, as he talks of "the obstinacy of my case".[7] But James's "case" was essentially behind his symptoms, in their unaccountable, unconscious source. It is this private value — quietly attaching itself to the public lexical item — that makes for its remarkable insistence in his writing. For the word "case" lost its semantic innocence very early in James's career.

In July 1866, the *Atlantic Monthly* published anonymously in its opening pages "The Case of George Dedlow", a story by Silas Weir Mitchell, the later eminent neurologist.[8] (Many years

---

[7] *Henry James: Letters*, ed. Leon Edel, 4 vols, Cambridge: Mass. and London, 1974-84, I, 224, 207.

[8] For the text of "The Case of George Dedlow", see Appendix. Silas Weir Mitchell was born into a medical family in Philadelphia in 1829. After an early period of medical and physiological research (into, *inter alia*, the crystalography of haemoglobin, and rattlesnake venom), Weir Mitchell became an acting assistant surgeon in the Union Army, an experience out of which grew his *Gunshot Wounds and Other Injuries of Nerves* (1864), later to bring him fame as *Injuries to Nerves and Their Consequences* (1872) for his contribution to the understanding of the peripheral nerves. Mitchell's research interests remained many and varied, and were both clinical and laboratory based. He continued through a long and energetic life to make original contributions to knowledge in many fields. These included a major contribution to therapeutics in his much-translated *Fat and Blood* (1877) with its celebrated if controversial advocacy of the place of rest (together with massage, overfeeding, electrotherapy and physiotherapy) in the treatment of functional nervous disorders. It is, of course, for this "rest cure" that he is now most remembered. (Henry James's Sussex physician William Osler had earlier been one Mitchell's assistant in Philadelphia and tried his mentor's rest cure on James in 1910 until his patient revolted.) Despite his prodigiously active medical life, Weir Mitchell found time for a parallel literary career in which he figured as a poet, a novelist — author, notably, of *Roland Blake* (1886), *Hugh Wynne*,

afterwards, in 1905, James was to meet him in Philadelphia, as a friend of Edith Wharton.[9]) Mitchell had served as an assistant surgeon in the Union army and had made a special study of nerve injuries. It was out of this experience that his first medical texts — and this story — were to come. Now, the young Henry James had first published in the *Atlantic* in March of the previous year (1865) and was to place two stories there in 1867 and three in 1868. It seems certain that, surveying his market and competitors, he would have read "The Case of George Dedlow" as a matter of course. At any rate, the most interesting of James's contributions to the magazine in 1868 was called "A Most Extraordinary Case", the story of a Civil War veteran suffering a mysterious affliction. When we consider the details of publication, it is difficult not to see in James's title a deliberate — and perhaps depreciating — allusion to Mitchell's story. For there is no doubt that the earlier story also proposed itself as an "extraordinary case", and that the lurid, gruesome and supernatural elements in it would have struck James as crude and amateurish. (It was certainly as an amateur of fiction that James treated Mitchell in 1905.) And so he "replied", with his own subtler variety of the extraordinary; though he unwittingly took from Mitchell's story much more than he knew.

The history of George Dedlow was essentially a fictionalized medical case history in which the sufferings of a young military protagonist were rendered so grimly unmysterious that the *Atlantic* was to receive donations to support him. In the course of the "autobiographical" narrative, Dedlow loses in turn each of his limbs, until he is reduced to a human stump. In the end, so much of his body is missing that his sense of personal identity becomes threatened:

> About one half of the sensitive surface of my skin was gone and thus much of relation to the outer world destroyed .... Moreover, all the great central ganglia, which give rise to movements in the limbs, were also eternally at rest. Thus one

---

Free Quaker (1898) and *Constance Trescott* (1905) — and as a writer of short stories. "The Case Of George Dedlow" (1866) was his first published story. Silas Weir Mitchell died in 1914.

[9] *Life*, II, 580-81.

> half of me was absent or functionally dead. This set me to thinking how much a man might lose and yet live .... I concluded that ... if utter loss of relation to the outer world were capable of destroying a man's consciousness of himself, the destruction of half of his sensitive surfaces might well occasion, in a less degreee, a like result, and so diminish his sense of individual existence.[10]

There is no doubt that, in 1866, part of the interest of the story was medical, lying in Mitchell's novel documentation of the (now relatively familiar) sensory hallucination known as phantom limb. The young veteran does not merely suffer grotesque physical mutilation, but is plagued by painful sensations in the limbs that he no longer has. No mystification of this is admitted to the narrative, however: such sensation is explained in terms of residual neural activity at the sites of amputation. Thus the history of this sad "fraction of a man"[11] is not exalted above the grizzly catalogue of facts out of which it is composed.

I cannot forbear to speculate on the impression that this strange tale must have made on the twenty three year old future novelist. It is true that, unlike Mitchell, he addressed the topic of war veterans without the direct experience of combat. For, as is well-known, a solicitous Henry James Snr had contrived the exemption of his clever elder boys from the Civil War, though his younger sons, Bob and Wilky, did enlist and see action, Wilky returning wounded from the assault on Fort Wagner to the family home at Newport in July 1863. But, on the other hand, there can be no doubt that — within this suggestive family setting — Henry James was living in these years with the trauma of his own private (if phantasmal) war. For, as is also well-known, in the spring of 1861, just as the great national conflict erupted, Henry suffered the "obscure hurt" to his lumbar region that was destined to fill

---

[10] "The Case of George Dedlow", *The Atlantic Monthly*, XVIII/105 (July 1866), 1-11, 8. I have reproduced the text of this story as an appendix.

[11] *Ibid.*, 11.

the office of more palpable wounds.[12] Whatever its physical basis, this "hurt" did not lack an emotional and psychical reality. Such a view may readily be married to Henry's later account of this fratricidal conflict in which he feared for "what might still happen, to everyone about me": "almost any tension would do, would serve for one's share" in the convulsions of the "enclosing social body, a body rent with a thousands wounds".[13] (One is reminded also of William's later theory of sympathetic muscular participation in a remote event.)

It is, therefore, not James's likely technical disdain for "The Case of George Dedlow" that intrigues me, so much as the things the story must have said to him, the invisible ways in which it must have solicited his imagination, beneath the stern vigilance of taste and opinion. For imagination has no ears to stop up against the secret gasp of recognition. However he may have considered "The Case of George Dedlow" a shabby affair, artistically speaking, it was, I believe, from the seed of Mitchell's half man that James's own "Extraordinary Case" was to grow. Not, of course, to begin: for the psychic business transacted there did not spring into being in James's early twenties. But Mitchell's story supplied an important element to James's imagination, by investing it — irresistibly — with an image that it recognized, an image that arrived as if it were merely returning. For, as we have seen, the fantasy of personal mutilation was already an insistent and unquiet element in James's unconscious thought, and it is to be presumed that it craved a means of discharge in representation. Accordingly, when James's early story "A Most Extraordinary Case" assembles itself, with impeccable unconscious logic, around its hero's grim mathematical lament ("It takes more than half a man to fall in love."[14]), we should hear the plaintif voice of George Dedlow, that other fractional man, echoing behind it.

But on the other hand we should not allow this family resemblance to mask an important distinction, for James's tale is,

---

[12] *Autobiography*, 415.

[13] *Ibid.*

[14] *Tales*, I, 237.

in its essential matter, a literal mirror image of Mitchell's: it does not merely reflect but also inverts its source. The strange fate of George Dedlow is to be haunted by phantoms of the body he no longer has, by fantasies of wholeness , if one will; James's afflicted soldier has a body whose actual wholeness does not protect him from fantasies of its mutilation. Or indeed of its decease: it is a "miserable carcass", not quite in life. For, one indication of the oddity of James's tale, is that we need to keep reminding ourselves, as we read, that his "young invalid officer" actually bears no visible wound. The physical ground of his malady is, to say the least, elusive, — as elusive, indeed, as any frank or unequivocating account of its severity. For, although the "disorder" is "deeply seated" and "virulent", it asks no stronger medicine than "unflinching care and prudence" to "subdue" it.[15]

It is difficult to read these details without being sent back to the pages in James's autobiography where the "obscure hurt" of 1861 is anatomized. It is the same ambivalent estimate of the gravity of a wound that dictates the choice of epithet: so the event is a "difficulty", a "mishap" or a "catastrophe", the product of a "soft spring" or a "dark hour" — and

> it was only a mystification the more that the inconvenience of my state had to reckon with the strange fact of there being nothing to speak of the matter with me.[16]

Clearly, it is unnecessary to labour the intimate relation of Ferdinand Mason to the troubled imagination that devised his strange history. Nor is it difficult to contrast Mason rather sharply with the "case" of his more tangibly afflicted fictional brother, George Dedlow. But at bottom the niceties of parallel and contrast belong to the discourse that we are attempting to deconstruct. It is perhaps more important to see that in Frederick Mason we are dealing with someone whose experience amounts to the psychical equivalent[17] of actual physical mutilation. His

---

[15] *Ibid.*, 233, 227.

[16] *Autobiography*, 417.

[17] *The Language of Psychoanalysis*, 363-64.

invisible wound is, after all, one to which he actually succumbs: his psychical reality is more potent than the discernible physical facts. He thus takes an assured place among the unconscious anatomical fantasies of his creator.

It is interesting that "A Most Extraordinary Case" begins with the therapeutic intervention of a woman, the young soldier's aunt, who promises to cure him in a month, if he consents to let himself be taken, a convalescent, to her home in the country. She finds him "in one of the uppermost chambers" of a New York Hotel, and rapidly installs him in a chamber "designedly on the ground floor" of her home, which lies "directly on the river".[18] Oddly, however, this well-intentioned removal inaugurates a chain of events that costs young Mason his life, and it is on this therapeutic paradox ("It's the most extraordinary case I ever heard of. The man was steadily getting well."[19]) that the story turns. Clearly we must try to reach some understanding of the crisis provoked in this "war wasted young officer" by what appears to be an unequivocal improvement in his "circumstances".

The fact is, that the detail of the lady's attention to Mason's "circumstances" deserves some scrutiny. That his aunt should find him in a high and solitary hotel room and supply for his relief a domestic alternative, "designedly" on the ground floor, may be taken as a fine and eminently practical measure. But it involves also — in addressing itself to the issue of the high and the low — an implicit (and quite unconscious) mapping of the soldier's body. (The representational device is one that we are already familiar with from my previous chapter.) We must not lose sight of the fact that we are reading a tale that Henry James wrote after a war that had helped to impair his sense of himself (his "egoistic sentiment of individuality", as George Dedlow would say[20]), a tale whose words and images, however unremarkable, are secretly

---

[18] *Tales*, I, 225, 231, 229.

[19] *Ibid.*, 260.

[20] "The Case of George Dedlow", 8.

touched with unconscious fantasy, and must therefore be placed in the discourse of his unconscious. This being so, we must neither read too literally nor fail to read literally enough. "I've no doubt it's more than half your circumstances", Mason's aunt reassuringly remarks of his illness — a remark for which we could devise a dozen innocent contexts, but which here seems to steal a rapid glance at the vexed anatomical issue, the "more than half a man" that, according to the Mason's own formula, it takes to fall in love.[21] At first sight, the lady may indeed find him "a great full-blown young fellow"; but the evidence for that view of him is exhausted in the remark itself, to whose fulsome heartiness rereading lends almost a wicked irony.[22] Wherever we look, this tale has no true focus of interest but the "miserable carcass" of Ferdinand Mason. It is both the restoration of and his restoration to that abandoned body, his rescue from the dull grey prison of high cerebration, that his installation on the ground floor "directly on the river" has in view. In short, it is the hope of an assumption of manhood that is held out to him by that place. And the point is also made in a more conventional fashion: for a beautiful young woman also watches over his convalescence.

We need not abuse ourselves with misapprehensions: before the story ends the young woman will be the wife of Dr Knight, the unmysterious chivalric antitype of Ferdinand. (William James was to complete his medical degree in June of 1869.) This *miles gloriosus* wins his lady in a brave and bloodless campaign. It is not, however, the means of his winning but of Ferdinand's losing that principally concerns us. Two ladies coax the invalid towards health: an elder and a younger, the type of mother and sweetheart respectively. To the "mother", this new bedside care is to be the re-enactment of a childhood illness through which she had formerly nursed him. It is of some significance that, whatever Ferdinand's imputed military character, the passive or supine side of this relation — the role of patient — is one that he meets with "delicious submission": he does not merely surrender to the

---

[21] *Tales*, I, 228.

[22] *Ibid*.

"dominion of women" but to their "uncontested dominion".[23] As James later remarked, the "supine attitude" in which he passed the troubled war years felt like the very "negative of combat".[24]

The additional details here — that Ferdinand's illness in some way repeats an earlier one; and, that his experience of being ill is not altogether unpleasurable — also invite some comment. (They indicate attitudes that we shall encounter elsewhere in James, and that will emerge, indeed, as family characteristics.) To be ill is to invite care; and this care is so precious that it is elicited, commemorated and reenacted in later illness. In these conditons, the process of coaxing a patient towards health is likely to be fraught with dangers. The danger, for example, of the patient's addiction to illness, of his finding in sickness the readiest path to care — and out of other difficulties. And the path also, through physical attentions, to a safe ("uncontested") and regressively legitimized eroticizing of the body. Whatever the other psychical determinants of Ferdinand's curious disposition of spirit, it is also through the labyrinth of such considerations as these that those who wait on him (or try to understand him) must pick their way. They must be kind and yet not help to kill with their kindness.

We expect a tale of illness to concern itself with bodies and to be well furnished with anatomical images. In the strange history of Ferdinand Mason, James's fictional representative, who lies under the care of women, the anatomical image that predominates is unquestionably that of hands. "From this moment you are in my hands", announces Mrs Mason in the hotel room, as Ferdinand, as if already in wonderful imaginary submission, watches her "drawing on her gloves". We are not surprised that when she leaves he cries "like a homesick school boy".[25] Even with this, Ferdinand has by no means exhausted the regressive role that his matronly nurse holds out to him:

> The neighbourhood offered an interminable succession of beautiful drives; and poor Ferdinand took a truly exquisite pleasure

---

[23] *Ibid.*, 231.

[24] *Autobiography*, 417.

[25] *Tales*, I, 230.

> in reclining idly upon a pile of cushions, warmly clad, empty-handed, silent, with only his eyes in motion, and rolling rapidly between fragrant hedges and springing crops, and beside the outskirts of woods, and along the heights which overlooked the river.[26]

With this the vestments of manhood that have hung expectantly in the wings may be returned without risk to "Wardrobe". Here the infantilization of Ferdinand Mason is complete, as the phaeton becomes now a perambulator, in which our half-man succumbs to the seductions of a time before speech and thought and independent locomotion.

It may be imagined that such triumphant temporal regressions do little to advance our young soldier's suit with Miss Hofmann. Indeed, when we anatomize his relations with her, the younger of his two nurses, we find that the infantile role is not sucessfully abdicated. For one thing, the imagery of hands or handling persists both in metaphor ("she has [her life] quite in her own hands"), and in actuality, as the invalid's mute admiration of her person selects for special notice "her magnificent hands".[27] There persists too, as the secret meaning of this imagery, the same regressive fantasy of infantile helplessness and exquisite maternal superintendence that disclosed itself in Ferdinand's outings with Mrs Mason:

> "I'm no companion," he said. "I don't pretend to be one. I sit here deaf and dumb, and blind and halt, patiently waiting to be healed, waiting till this vagabond nature of ours strolls my way, and brushes me with the hem of her garment."[28]

Clearly, it would be a nice issue to determine which of the ladies is treated to the more thorough-going maternal identification, for a consistent distinction between the offices of wife and mother is one that Mason cannot sustain. But it is in relation to Caroline Hofmann that this remarkably consistent imagery of hands is

---

[26] Ibid., 237.

[27] Ibid., 236, 238.

[28] Ibid., 238.

pressed into fullest service. It is, in fact, allowed to usher in a minor crisis for the invalid, on an evening when the ladies purpose dancing and he an early bed. Before they leave, he watches "their slow assumption of their gloves" and undertakes to button those of the younger lady. When he is alone, "a pair of rejected gloves" graces the table and bears mute witness to what has been and is to be. There follows for him a

> sudden sensation, which cannot be better described than as a general collapse, He felt dizzy, faint, and sick. His head swam and his knees trembled.[29]

It is difficult to ignore the agency of the "rejected gloves" in this mysterious accession of weakness, however we choose to read the relation. They are perhaps best viewed, in their emptiness, as the pitiful phantoms of Mason's own all-but-useless hands. Simultaneously, they recall the absent ladies, whose support for the invalid in their hands is temporarily intermitted. If the veiled logic of his collapse is thus compelling, the incident is typical of the process by which the tale proceeds. The story is, indeed, essentially a succession of physical postures and attitudes, which — once we have an eye for them — insist to the point of impugning the innocence of the tale's words, that strive, unavailingly, to locate the performance in the light of day. "I wish to get well, on the whole", announces Mason.[30] But his creator's shrewd dissection of a perversity of the (invalid) will ("on the whole", but not altogether) draws in its train such charged and obsessive images of fragmentation and lost physical integrity that they seem almost to mock the domestic drama with their mutely surrealistic intrusions. James's house of fiction is here, as always, an externalization of the mind before it is a plausible representation of the world's concrete actualities. It has no address. His is an imagination and an art caught in the snares of an unconscious drama that does not merely stand at its source but unremittingly sustains it. The art of Henry James is, as we have seen, an art of minimal sublimation, an art that can never raise

---

[29] *Ibid.*, 242, 244.

[30] *Ibid.*, 249.

itself into impersonality. It is situated in a strange twilight borderland, where fiction haltingly begins and where the demons of neurosis first turn away from the encroaching daylight. This is not the tangible world of Balzac or Dickens, however it may strive on occasion to resemble it. For James gives us a world peopled by characters who convincingly assume the vestments of reality and yet, in the end, do not so much exist as signify. It is a world peopled by "cases".

In the opening pages of the "Extraordinary Case", this story that lies more or less at the beginning of James's career, Mrs Mason delivers an ominous word: "I shall of course", she says, "meet you at your journey's end".[31] These words may be taken as doubly prophetic, for, aside from the fact that she here foretells Mason's death, there is indeed another story, a late one, in which she keeps her promise (and the rendezvous), thereby oddly satisfying the symmetry of things, and serving to confirm the persistence and continuity of certain issues in James's imagination. Forty years after the narrative of Ferdinand Mason, Henry James published "The Jolly Corner" (1908), one of the fruits of his visit to the United States at the beginning of the new century. Appropriately, it is the story of a man, Spencer Brydon, who, in his declining years, recrosses an ocean to revisit the scene of his childhood and youth. But his essential business is neither commercial nor social but spectral. In his empty but preserved ancestral home, it is his curious occupation to nightly pace the floors and wander the corridors in search of his alternative self, the superior man (he is convinced) he might have been, had he stayed in his native land. Success does not elude him, and the climax of the story is a strange nocturnal confrontation with the apparitional stranger he seeks. At this awesome moment, Brydon has time to register some curious physical details in his prey ("one of these hands had lost two fingers, which were reduced to stumps, as if accidently shot away"), but then "as under the hot

---

[31] *Ibid.*, 230.

breath and the roused passion of a life larger than his own," he feels "his very feet give way" and collapses.[32]

"Alice Staverton arrives to rescue him from his fainting spell", comments Leon Edel.[33] There are, in fact, as in the earlier story, two women to assist him in his crisis, but it is — in my view — the office of neither to "rescue" him from it. We are not surprised that they are a younger (the spinster) and an elder (the housekeeper), though, measuring time from "A Most Extraordinary Case", their ages have kept pace, proportionately, with that of the protagonist. The ladies are necessary for the precise (psychic) orchestration of Brydon's collapse, a fact that the story frankly confesses: it was "as if his prodigious journey had been all for the sake of it".[34] For if the dreadful meeting with the ghost is the climax of this tale, the meaning of that crisis cannot be divorced from the resultant swoon in which the brideless hero falls into the delicious care of women.

We note, first of all, that they tend him on the floor, whose familiar and remembered black and white marble tiles restore him to an earlier childhood world. Female faces appear and bend over him as he lies mutely looking up. He is conscious of a "tenderness of support" and of his head "pillowed in extraordinary softness" on the lap of Alice Staverton. He feels he has been

> miraculously *carried* back — lifted and carefully borne as from where he had been picked up, the utmost end of an interminable grey passage .... He must moreover, with intermissions, still have been lifted and borne; since why and how else should he have known himself, later on, with the afternoon glow intenser, no longer at the foot of his stairs — situated as these now seemed at the dark other end of his tunnel — but on a deep window-bench of his high saloon, over which had been spread, couch-fashion, a mantle of soft stuff lined with grey fur that was familiar to his eyes and that one of his hands kept fondly feeling as for its pledge of truth. Mrs Muldoon's face

---

[32] *Henry James: Stories of the Supernatural*, ed. Leon Edel, London, 1971, 756.

[33] *Life*, II, 620.

[34] *Henry James: Stories of the Supernatural*, 757.

> had gone, but the other, the second he had recognised, hung over him in a way that showed how he was still propped and pillowed. He took it all in, and the more he took it the more it seemed to suffice: he was as much at peace as if he had had food and drink.[35]

We have to remind ourselves that the delicious passivity of this is a creative lifetime away from the fantasies of Ferdinand Mason. Yet, awesomely, the inner clock stands still at the same moment. For here Brydon is not merely revisiting the scene of his childhood and youth but has fallen into a fantasy of infancy. We may judge the strength of the fantasy — the strength of the lure to temporal regression — by the sensory elaboration of the infantile imagery, which seems to extend even to a tentative reprise of the physical experience of birth.

We have, up to this point, given little consideration to the masculine side of this experience, to the terror that forces Brydon to "give ground" before the "evil, odious, blatant, vulgar" stranger who had "advanced for aggression":

> Then harder pressed still, sick with the force of his shock, and falling back as under the hot breath and the roused passion of a life larger than his own, a rage of personality before which his own collapsed, he felt the whole vision turn to darkness and his very feet give way.[36]

There are very good reasons for comparing this ghostly meeting in "The Jolly Corner" with the confrontation in the dream of the Louvre that we considered in the previous chapter. In fact, such a comparison was evidently present to James himself:

> The most intimate idea of "The Jolly Corner" is that my hero's adventure there takes the form so to speak of his turning the tables, as I think I called it, on a "ghost" or whatever, a visiting or haunting apparition otherwise qualified to appal him; and thereby winning a sort of victory by the appearance, and the

---

[35] *Ibid.*, 757-58.

[36] *Ibid.*, 756-57.

evidence, that this personage or presence was more overwhelmingly affected by him than he by it.[37]

In his editorial remarks, Professor Edel does not fail to point out the striking inaccuracy of this, as the triumph over the noctural intruder in the Louvre dream is speciously extended to cover defeat by the mutilated ghostly stranger in the tale. (James, he observes, had evidently more courage in dream than he could muster in fictions manufactured by daylight.) But the trick of memory here is intriguing. James confused the two scenarios because, whatever their outward differences, they shared an essential dream-core. We may surmise that, in each case, the outcome is governed by the wishful infantile fantasy directing the performance. The triumph of the dream — as the intruder "flies for his life" — is clear enough; but what analogous "triumph" crowns the story?

The reader's liability to interpret the climax of "The Jolly Corner" as the notation of a defeat demonstrates the problems that flow from not reading literally enough in texts of psychic manufacture. For the threat of the mutilated (and presumably mutilating) stranger is averted by Brydon's faint: here the vulnerable sleeping figure wakes up to no horror but to exquisite female care. The stranger is nowhere to be seen: and this absence marks *his* annihilation. The psychic structure of the Louvre dream persists here, if not to the word yet to the letter. In fact, it would be difficult to exaggerate the shared parentage of the dream and the story — in their familial character, for example. Indeed, "The Jolly Corner" is in some respects so familial that, oddly for James, it becomes almost a private communication. "Alice" was certainly a family name — the name of William's wife and that of his beloved younger sister, now long dead. Father is also present: the mutilated fingers, recalling the elder Henry's amputation, and the "roused passion of a life larger than his own" his unvanquished potency, clearly send us back to the Oedipal conflict that is part of the Louvre dream. But it is, above all, that the fictional Alice should know of the "stranger"'s mutilation

---

[37] *Ibid.*, 724.

without being told that confers the secret mark of consanguinity on the phantoms of the tale.

In fact, Professor Edel is very far from making "The Jolly Corner", considered as a whole, the site of a defeat. For if the ghost "overwhelms" Spencer Brydon, he will wake up to the assurance that the awful mutilated stranger is not himself, in any allowable sense. And Edel notes also how James proceeds from this story to a final decade of striving and achieving, with the ghost of his other self (we are to believe) consummately banished. Now it is certainly true that the final (or rebirth) section of "The Jolly Corner" achieves a note of authentic if rueful triumph. But it is by no means the triumph of "active and masculine" striving. It is the triumph of a prodigious fantasy of regression, of retreat from the arena of relational conflict in which battles may be lost, or engaged with fearsome risks. Here is yet another war fought in the "supine attitude" that is the "negative of combat". There is simply no escaping the fact that Brydon's conflict with the mutilated stranger is, in the first instance, a defeat: "I can only have died" he moans to Alice Staverton, "You brought me literally to life".[38] In the moments before Brydon's fantastic rebirth, the space between chapters in which he is "gone", it is hard to make the lying figure into an image of triumph. We are more likely to see in him the "nervous prostration" that will shortly haunt his ageing creator. Or to see the infantilized Frederick Mason. Brydon is thus as thoroughly and irretrievably a casualty as the young soldier whose infantilized state he mirrors, as extraordinary a case as he. For he dies in metaphor if not in fact.

This brings us to what is without doubt the deeper reason for James's blurring of the grandiose climax of his Louvre dream with the more dishonourable fate of the — essentially routed — Spencer Brydon. The issue of active (masculine) triumph as opposed to passive (feminine) defeat — an issue linked to the whole narcissistically urgent question of self-regard, personal efficacy and bodily integrity — lies at the core of both imaginative products. This means that James's misremembering of the tale — in

---

[38] Ibid., 758-59.

the active direction of triumph — is simply a wishful reversal, offered to consciousness, of unconscious misgivings. Derivatively, the question whether he is indeed a man of courage ("one of those types who have been hammered so hard and made so keen") presses throughout for Brydon and even precedes the ghost-hunt as he takes significant pleasure, for example, in his newly-discovered ability for "standing-up" to the "man in charge" of his building renovations. When he begins to stalk the sleeping ghost of the man he might have been, he does so at the outset with an active "rigour to which nothing in his life had been comparable".[39] The supreme representational skill of the tale lies, however, in the stealthy and insidious process by which, his courage in the great empty house gradually failing, the hero is able to continue to consider himself not afraid. So his trick of not reflecting on what does not suit his preferred view of himself (as, leaving the shutters open for the comfort of the streetlight), and so too the flourishingly masculine emphasis he choses to place on, for example, his visual acuity ("he gained to an extraordinary degree the power to penetrate the dusk"[40]). The near-comic fiction of his courage is one which he even manages to sustain when, coming at last on his elusive long-sought quarry behind a closed door, he forbears to open the door and affront the "black stranger" on the grounds of the (suddenly-grasped) higher value of "Discretion". The flight thus determined is never given its name, nor is the crucial place in it of the impression that the unseen "agent"[41] behind the door is defiantly standing his ground, undismayed.

The crucial lapse of his fragile courage in this contest between Brydon's wish "actively [to] inspire ... fear" and his liability "passively [to] know it" is determined by another circumstance that is worthy of comment. It occurs to him that, whereas in his hunt he favours the frontal reaches of the house, next to the street, his quarry's taste is quite other, is indeed for the "rear of

---

[39] Ibid., 736, 729, 741.

[40] Ibid., 742.

[41] Ibid., 761, 749, 748.

the house" — including an "ample back staircase" — which now affects him as "the very jungle of his prey". From these ideas come the twin impressions of ceasing to follow and of being followed, and then swiftly in the wake of these, the image of

> Pantaloon, at the Christmas farce, buffeted and tricked from behind by ubiquitous Harlequin; ...[42]

There can be little surprise in the fact that, at this juncture, the passive impression of being "sightless" and "kept in sight" is substituted for Brydon's erstwhile (actively) grandiose sense of "optical reach".[43] The fear (including the fear of humiliation) at the heart of this remarkable story is undoubtedly derived from James's earliest psychological experiences, which is why it finds ready (phase-appropriate) expression in anatomical fantasies, thinly disguised. Chief among these is a fear that perhaps provides the most vividly concrete expression of anxious passivity in a man: the fear of being penetrated from behind.[44] As I have suggested, at the innermost core of James's persisting unconscious preoccupations are conflicts over activity and passivity, over masculine and feminine identifications and the relation to persons that derive from these psychological positions. Whether we think

---

[42] *Ibid.*, 745, 743, 744.

[43] *Ibid.*, 743.

[44] The setting of the Louvre dream — the Galerie d' Apollon — sheds some unexpected light on this issue. James was very familiar from childhood with Bunyan's *Pilgrim's Progress* and makes frequent references to it in his critical writing. One of the most vivid and frightening sequences in Bunyan's remarkable work (which proposes itself, of course, as a dream or vision) is the phantasmagoric nocturnal contest between Christian and the destroying monster Apollyon. At the beginning of the contest, Christian realizes that his cannot flee, for his back is unprotected and would be easily penetrable. Correspondingly, in the dream, we have the door that threatens to open inwards. It is very possible that the ostensibly Napoleonic setting of James's dream was overdetermined by memories of Bunyan.

of "A Most Extraordinary Case" (or of a late story such as "The Beast in the Jungle"), the (conscious or unconscious) longing that something happen to him, that something be done to him or for him, places the hero in a position "abysmally passive" (feminine) before other objects.[45] These include, in all cases, a triumphing masculine object. Conversely, the precarious assumption of a masculine position cannot be sustained in direct "mutilating" contest with another man's "larger life". For it is of the first importance that Brydon's ghost not be one intact and invulnerable but carry the intimidating stigmata of physical conflict: that is, he embodies "corroborating" fantasies of what may happen to a man and what may be done to you by a man, fantasies that, whatever the verifiable physical facts, had a deep psychical reality to Henry James.

The further clarification of this crucial matter, which finds what is undoubtedly its most illuminating fictional representation in *The Turn of the Screw*, must wait until the next chapter. But it would be unfortunate to leave the reader with the impression (readily formed, when it is an issue of pathology) that the psychological constellation we are gradually uncovering had only negative implications for Henry James and must always lead back to the question of what he suffered. For we can make here an important positive point in relation to that same pathology. What has become recognised as the peculiarly Jamesian attitude to experience, the deeply characteristic habit of minute and elaborate appreciation, is in essence also a passivity before the fact of experience itself and a subtle deferral of activity. But this way of taking the world, or, strictly, of being taken by it, was the immediate source of most of James's pleasure in human life. That it simultaneously led away from a vigorous engagement with the actual does not change this simple fact.

Such, at any rate, seem to me to be the principal unconscious issues informing the stories we have been considering, and, of course, determining their outcomes, — be it Brydon's swoon, Mason's swoon or Mason's more comprehensive capitulation. For how, in any case, are we to understand Ferdinand Mason's death

---

[45] *Ibid.*, 757.

if not as a metaphorical protraction of his swoon, the further falling-away of manhood, all evidence of a wound that cannot be seen or felt and yet breaks the man? As I have sufficiently indicated, Dr Knight survives the baffling young soldier and wins the lady. But even his triumph is not unqualified: we must find a moment to pity the scientist who vainly hoped to view a hurt so obscure:

> [Dr Knight] would have given a great deal to have been able to make an autopsy.[46]

---

[46] *Tales*, I, 261.

4

Autopsy

> What happens between two, and between all the "two's" one likes, such as between life and death, can only *maintain itself* with some ghost, can only *talk with* or *about* some ghost.
>
> Jacques Derrida, *Specters of Marx* (1994).

It is not for nothing that *The Turn of the Screw* has attracted more psychoanalytic attention than anything else that James wrote.[1] Even without the benefit of a psychoanalytic training, the average reader is likely to have a powerful intuition of extraordinary and murky psychological depths in the piece. No need here to get behind the veneer of polite drawing rooms and elaborate cerebration to the unconscious core, for *The Turn of the Screw* reads like the relatively undistorted unconscious communication that it actually is. By this I mean that its manifest topics and persons have proceeded no great distance from their latent or

---

[1] Out of a considerable and diverse literature see, for example, Edmund Wilson, "The Ambiguity of Henry James" in *The Triple Thinkers*, New York, 1952; M. Katan, "A Causerie on Henry James's *The Turn of the Screw*", in *The Psychoanalytic Study of the Child*, XVII (1962), 473-93; M. Katan, "The Origin of *The Turn of the Screw*", in *The Psychoanalytic Study of the Child*, XXI (1966), 583-635; C. Brooke-Rose, *A Rhetoric of the Unreal*, Cambridge, 1981. The fullest psychoanalytic bibliography on *The Turn of the Screw* is to be found on CD-ROM: *Archive I* (1920-94), Psychoanalytic Electronic Publishing, Delaware, 1997.

instinctual sources. It is a question of congruence: the story fits its unconscious determinants like a glove.[2]

This means that what often opposes the successful or convincing psychoanalysis of art is not encountered here. For sometimes the original instinctual and infantile sources are so heavily disguised and their force so successfully attenuated that only an act of intellectual violence — involving flagrant reductionism or leaden implausibilities — can reestablish the appropriate lost links. It is indeed with the critic and his reader as it is with the psychoanalyst and his patient: the patient's conscious and reasonable ego cannot accept unconscious contents reached by a brutal frontal assault: these can only be arrived at and tolerated when the defensive processes of the ego are analysed and the ego thus made ready to receive them. By analogy, the reader of psychoanalytic criticism cannot see violence done to the ego-like outer rind of the work of art — its surface images and situations — without rebelling in some measure against the blind instrument conducting the investigation. But this important issue of tact and plausibility is perhaps more easily handled with James's famous "supernatural" text. For if displacements, condensations and overdeterminations abound in *The Turn of the Screw*, they are already clearly visible in the surface elements of the story and are not limited to the secret interplay of these elements with their hidden unconscious antecedents. The key ideas and feelings have not, that is, been banished to the periphery of the story, whose centre is thereby robbed of its instinctual charge and left blank and inscrutable to interpretation. In *The Turn of the Screw* James's unconscious speaks directly and in the most distinct tones imaginable:

> The limit of this evil time had arrived only when, on the dawn of a winter's morning, Peter Quint was found, by a labourer

---

[2] See chapter 6(D) ("Considerations of Representability") of Freud's *The Interpretation of Dreams*, in *The Complete Psychological Works of Sigmund Freud*, IV-V. The reader of these important pages in Freud — and of *The Interpretation of Dreams* as a whole — will be aware that this text has informed the approach adopted in the present study more than any other work.

going to early work, stone dead on the road from the village: a catastrophe explained — superficially at least — by a visible wound to his head; such a wound as might have been produced (and as, on the final evidence, *had* been) by a fatal slip, in the dark and after leaving the public-house, on the steepish icy slope, a wrong path altogether, at the bottom of which he lay. The icy slope, the turn mistaken at night and in liquor, accounted for much — practically, in the end and after the inquest and boundless chatter, for everything; but there had been matters in his life, strange passages and perils, secret disorders, vices more than suspected, that would have accounted for a good deal more.[3]

This is the most visible corpse, the most clearly advertised and examinable dead body in James's work. It is appropriate that we should find it in *The Turn of the Screw* (1898), for it is here, in his first dictated story, that James's lifelong unconscious concern with the body becomes finally irrepressible. Here his unconscious is clamorous for representation, and finds it in images more troubled and fantastic than any we can meet elsewhere in his fiction. As we shall see, there are good reasons for concluding that the spectacle of Quint's dead body is the heart of the tale, and not simply as that body lies here in all evidence, but as it offers itself to view at other special moments. (And let us not forget that a lifeless male form — Miles, dead in the arms of his governess — is also the last image of the story.) Quint's body holds the key to this fictional labyrinth, and that is why we should come to *The Turn of the Screw* as to an autopsy — to consider the body and establish the cause of death of Peter Quint — an enterprise into which the quoted passage teasingly draws us. There is no deeper "well of unconscious cerebration"[4] than that out of which rises this ghostman — in life "not quite in health", in death not quite

---

[3] Henry James: *The Turn of the Screw*, ed. R. Kimbrough, New York, 1966, 28.

[4] *The Art of the Novel: Critical Prefaces*, ed. R. P. Blackmur, New York, 1934, 23.

extinct.⁵ In the figure of Peter Quint lie locked the closest secrets of James's imagination.

In all of his (mostly spectral) embodiments we will find complications and oddities. The passage that tells us of Quint's death is as slippery as his path home. "A clear unextraordinary case", says one voice; "More to this death than meets the eye", says another. Considering the scene of his death, it is hard not to recall that, to the "haunted" governess, in his first appearance, the apparitional Quint — strutting and fretting on the crenellated tower — resembled nothing so much as an actor;⁶ and that, to her also, autumnal Bly

> with its grey sky and withered garlands, its bared spaces and scattered dead leaves, was like a theatre after the performance — all strewn with crumpled playbills.⁷

Accordingly, we can almost smell the spirit of the theatre in Quint's cheap catastrophe — that is what is wrong with the perfidious net of words that covers his corpse. There is an all-too-evident attempt to present his body and the story of what has become of it with irreproachable clarity. It is as if bold forensic chalk-marks have already mapped the site and point to the head-wound that is to explain all things. But nothing is clear here — except the attempt at clarity. The words do not tell so much as they serve to draw us into a maze — offering, now a certainty quickly punctured, now a doubt hastily suppressed. Certainty about what happened to Quint is at one moment lavishly offered, at the next shabbily withdrawn. And the extraordinary passage ends with an additional convolution: not only may the facts not explain the body but the body may be more in need of explaining than appears. What perversity of explanation is this, making us doubt an assurance that there is no doubt? What game, to present facts, call them conclusive, yet refuse to conclude? Assuredly the death of Peter Quint is no simple affair.

---

5   *The Turn of the Screw*, 27.

6   Ibid., 24.

7   Ibid., 52.

But whatever mysteries, whatever anatomical puzzles may be enclosed there, it is noteworthy that the body of Peter Quint is not the first to claim our attention in *The Turn of the Screw*. That distinction belongs to his "victim", to the newly-arrived young governess, whose first act in her room as Bly is to consider

> the long glasses in which, for the first time, I could see myself from head to foot.[8]

This moment — that of the governess's brief hesitation before the mirror — is not least remarkable for coming and going without insistence. For, properly understood, the business transacted in it is truly momentous. But a perverse rhetoric, — a rhetoric that underlines what may be discounted and passes in an instant what is crammed with rich seeds — a displacing rhetoric is one of the most persistent characteristics of *The Turn of the Screw*. If the laws of the piece were not thus dictated by the evasions and obfuscations of the unconscious, if the author had here possessed his art rather than been possessed by it, if *The Turn of the Screw* had belonged, for example, to the artificial but daylight world of opera, this moment would doubtless have swollen to an aria before the mirror. For it is both a beginning and an end. The beginning is clear, if surprising: a young girl sees the full extent of her body in a mirror, for the first time in her life. (As if to reiterate the anatomical point, she notes too the "figured full draperies" of her room.) Giver her love-interest in the Master, her employer, here is a moment of imaginary initiation, a moment announcing womanhood and physical maturation, a moment of delight. Artistically too it is a beginning, for a motif enters the story here: the image of the *complete* body.

But this beginning is also an end. What she sees no one will see again. The complete body, thus ritually presented, now leaves the stage, never to reappear. If, in retrospect, we can call this moment the announcing of a motif, it is one destined to be commemorated by its own absence. For if the banished phrase does not return whole, it insinuates itself in quiet fragments that secretly harp on its dismemberment. This amounts to saying that,

---

[8] *Ibid.*, 7.

in the matter of imagery, *The Turn of the Screw* is a haunted story — over and above its status as the story of a haunting. Artistically and psychically, it is haunted by the image of an incomplete (or damaged) human body — that is to say, by the body of Peter Quint. In common with the governess, we aready suspect that Quint is an actor; already we guess at his role: to "fill a vacancy" indeed — to fake anatomical completeness.

But here we presume, or at best anticipate, for our dead man lying by the roadside seemed complete enough. It is not empty clothing that is found in the cold dawn but the body of a man. And is it not the case, moreover, that the dead Quint appears to the governess — stands before her — on more than one occasion? It is true that (as Mrs Grose tells us) his haunting outfit is not his own;[9] but have we any warrant for assuming that it drapes a mere fragment of a man? Let us consider Peter Quint's second appearance:

> The person looking straight in was the person who had already appeared to me. He appeared thus again with I won't say greater distinctness, for that was impossible, but with a nearness that represented a forward stride in our intercourse and made me, as I met him, catch my breath and turn cold. He was the same — he was the same and seen, this time, as he had been seen before, from the waist up, the window, though the dining-room was on the ground floor, not going down to the terrace on which he stood.[10]

There are variations of place and circumstance in the ghostly appearances of Peter Quint, but they have all in common the remarkable and consistent fact that Quint displays himself only from the waist upwards. His full physical extent is never seen: he appears incomplete(ly). This remains true even in circumstances which present greater representational difficulties than his appearance on the tower or outside the dining-room window. For example, it is the same anatomical story when the governess encounters Quint on the stairs of the sleeping house. Above looking down, she notes that Quint reaches only "half-way up",

---

[9] *Ibid.*, 24.

[10] *Ibid.*, 20.

finding himself "stopped short". In the circumstances, the physical and representational difficulties of the intruder's retreat — "cut off" not merely in metaphor — this difficulty is covered decorously enough by a syntax of cunning ambiguity, as the "figure" goes

> with my eyes on the villainous back that no hunch could more disfigure, straight down the staircase and into the darkness in which the next bend was lost.[11]

Two things are clear, therefore: first, that Quint is presented as a consistent anatomical image, and, second, that, conformably with the perverse rhetoric we have already identified, the character of that image is essentially secret. For Quint's deficiency is there to be inferred, but it is by no means insisted on. And it was precisely this insight that the stagey spectacle of the ex-valet's corpse with its florid display of a head-wound attempted to obstruct. There *is* a good deal to put us off our guard. For is it not suggested, after all, that Peter Quint was, while he lived, an incorrigible womanizer, sharing this characteristic with his Harley Street Master, who has "charming ways with women" and whose study is littered with sundry "trophies of the chase"?[12] Peter Quint, we are assured, sinned not by abstinence or incapacity but by excess. How may we square our ghostly pseudo-amorous remnant with such a man? Or how, in the fact of such a man, can we maintain our conception of Quint's anatomical deficiency? We appear to have worked ourselves into an intellectual impasse.

Happily, this difficulty is more apparent than real and a solution requires merely that we give due weight to the unconscious determinants of the story. Chief among these is the clearly-inferable fact that the body of Peter Quint rose out of a special place in the unconscious fantasy, the unconscious image-making faculty of his creator. It is this that the secret consistency of his anatomy proclaims. And it is this which dictates the teasing reversals of the whole performance. For there is a kind of fiction that is content to flirt with its unconscious determinants, content

---

[11] *Ibid.*, 41.

[12] *Ibid.*, 4.

to rise into the daylight of representation and play there unburdened by the dark energy that lends it grace and power. More plainly said, fiction *can* sublimate its unconscious sources into a lucid and untroubled art: as Freud remarked, "Real art begins with the veiling of the unconscious".[13] But that is emphatically not James's fate in *The Turn of the Screw*. Here his imagination is ridden by the ghosts of his unconscious life, hounded and harried and pursued by them along the passages of the house of fiction. Here they brook no refusal; if he wants their power then they must be on stage with the people of daylight. It is out of this spectral company that Peter Quint emerges as the quintessential expression of James's imagination. But having made no truce with the powers of daylight, and "knowing" that his creator has here, in this ghostly tale, abandoned the fiction of social reality, Quint obeys, in this new place, the laws of the subliminal place he never ceases to inhabit. The unconscious world crosses over into the waking world of mankind in curious disguises. So Quint does not parade his ghastly lack but masquerades as a sexual adverturer: he represents himself as his opposite. To this unconscious witticism he adds a death fit for the theatre of melodrama. He lets is be known that he has died from a fall and a head-would. As if he were not in any case — in his "extraordinary case" — already essentially dead; as if *that* were the wound.

It is well-known and I have already recalled that, in the spring of 1861, at the outbreak of the American Civil War, in which he took no active part, Henry James suffered an injury that — in the most famous phrase of his autobiography — he called an "obscure hurt".[14] It is also well-known that, whatever the objective nature and severity of the (sacroiliac?) injury, it became the focus of a great deal of morbid psychological energy in the sufferer. But, above all, the incident appears to have set its seal upon what we

---

[13] *Minutes of the Vienna Psychoanalytic Society*, eds H. Nunberg and E. Federn, 4 vols, New York, 1962-75, II, 373.

[14] *Autobiography*, 415.

may call James's personal mythology, and to have done so by employing a mechanism that Sigmund Freud has characterized as follows:

> In persons who are disposed to be neurotic ... some morbid organic condition — perhaps an inflammation or an injury — very commonly sets the work of symptom-formation in motion; so that the latter process swiftly seizes upon the symptom supplied by reality, and uses it to represent those unconscious phantasies that have only been lying in wait for some means of expression.[15]

There is, as we are in the process of discovering, much evidence to suggest that, in his unconscious fantasy, Henry James had long thought of himself as one grievously injured, a man good as dead of an "obscure" wound, over which the spring of 1861 had drawn a too-careless finger. One of the things that we have in the portrait of Peter Quint, is a powerful imaginative representation of this important and persisting early fantasy of annulment and vanquished power that the incident in young adulthood found itself drawn into. It is the singular destiny of this ghostman, riddled with "secret disorders", to represent his creator with the most appalling intimacy. That is why the body of Quint is anatomized with such meticulous unconscious care and why we cannot consider it too curiously.

It was mostly suspicion that we brought away from our first consideration of the dead body of Peter Quint. The spectacle made us uneasy, taxed our credulity. On the other hand, there was some foolishness in expecting that the tale of a man "obscurely hurt" should be clear and unequivocal. Better to expect darkness or a specious clarity. And what but a misleading, perfidious clarity stares back at us from Quint's "visible wound to the head"? For here as everywhere in *The Turn of the Screw* the mechanisms of representation are those of the unconscious.[16]

---

[15] Sigmund Freud, *Introductory Lectures in Psychoanalysis*, in *The Complete Psychological Works of Sigmund Freud*, 24 vols, ed. James Strachey, London, 1953-74, XV-XVI, XVI, 391.

[16] See *The Interpretation of Dreams*, chapter 6, "The Dream-Work".

Thing change their names, change places, hide in their opposites. So the vagueness of a "hurt" takes refuge in the graphic determinateness of a "wound"; if the "hurt" was "obscure" the "wound" is not merely there but — oddly — "visible". But these displacements and inversions subserve another anatomical displacement that is the work's central strategy. We are asked to believe that his "deadness" is a matter of damage to the higher faculties only.

But if the governess does not *see* him from the waist down, she by no means ceases to meditate on the nature of his insufficiency — though, here again, the unremitting mechanism of displacement draws a plausible veil over her obsession. When she refers to Quint her remarks merely insist on the lowness of his social rank. So he is a "base menial"; on another occasion a "low wretch" provided (in a socio-moral pun) with a "villainous back".[17] These exceedingly vigorous remarks fall a little curiously from the mouth of "the youngest of several daughters of a poor country parson"[18] and seem to uncover an extraordinary social presumption. But it is interesting to notice that all her terms of derision are ambiguous, and ambiguous in the same way — by consistently admitting of a spatial meaning. The governess's obsessed emphasis is nothing other than a (convenient) displacement into the socio-moral of a preoccupation which is essentially anatomical. Thus her disapproval may both secretly and openly direct itself at the lower half of Quint's body.

Up to this point I have dwelt so exclusively on the deficiencies of Peter Quint, that anyone assembling an account of *The Turn of the Screw* from my words only, could be forgiven for making him out a quaking and pusillanimous ghost, remnant of the fraction of a man. And what I have said so far suggests (for the governess) mostly a tale of frustration and lovelessness. In this I have failed to convey the dominant feeling-tone of *The Turn of the Screw* and have neither addressed nor explained the pronounced elements of menace that give the story its considerable power. The Quint who haunts the corridors of Bly may be no sexual predator, but

---

[17] *The Turn of the Screw*, 36, 41.

[18] *Ibid.*, 4.

he is a fearful presence and a far-from-extinguished spirit. He is still a predator — after his fashion. We have seen that Peter Quint is apparently condemned to live only as a higher man, anatomically speaking. One way of formulating his menace is to observe that the "higher man" is not without compensating faculties, products, we might say, of a kind of demonic conversion. For the ghostly Quint has retained his predatory instincts, albeit that they have been displaced upwards. To what end does he come, but to look, to fix, to stare? In the ample gardens of Bly the governess acutely figures the "fellow" who was a "hound" now "prowling for a sight" — his new vice.[19]

It is, of course, difficult to make out an image of unequivocal potency in the stare of a Quint who "hungrily" hovers.[20] And if the erstwhile adventurer now preys with his eyes, his essential muteness seems but additional testimony to a predatory faculty that is severely curtailed. This wordless ghost is indeed a most paradoxical offspring of one who gave up his life to the curious and lonely rituals of verbal manufacture that hide behind the bland word "novelist". It is as if Quint's eyes have in some fashion usurped the office of his mouth, as if he suffers some inhibition of speech. How may we connect this characteristic with those of his voluble creator?

One of the things that *The Turn of the Screw* — uniquely — enables us to do, is to reconstruct phases of instinctual conflict in the early development of Henry James. I believe that it is possible to locate such a focus of neurotic development at the time when he was engaged on the acquisition of speech. We know a good deal about his adult speech: that it was slow, that it was elaborate, that it was full of pauses — to such phenomena we have heard numerous contemporary witnesses testify. As I have argued, these things were actually the persisting stigmata of infantile conditions. To press further into this issue, let us call up

---

[19] *Ibid.*, 33, 44.

[20] *Ibid.*, 46.

again the testimony of Edith Wharton whose great closeness to James in the last years of his life gives her words special authority. According to her, Henry's

> slow way of speech ... was really the partial victory over a stammer which in his boyhood had been thought incurable.[21]

This is a rare piece of evidence, but it is not impossible to find half-conscious reminiscences of the same state of affairs elsewhere — in William James's correspondence, for example. This is from a letter of 1907 that we have already glanced at:

> You know how opposed your whole "third manner" of execution is to the literary ideals which animate my crude and Orson-like breast, mine being to say a thing in one sentence as straight and explicit as it can be made, and then to drop it forever; yours being to avoid naming it straight, but by dint of breathing and sighing all round and round it, to arouse in the reader who may have had a similar perception already (Heaven help him if he hasn't!) the illusion of a solid object, made (like the "ghost" at the Polytechnic) wholly out of impalpable materials, air, and the prismatic inferences of light, ingeniously focussed by mirrors upon empty space .... But it's the rummest method for one to employ systematically as you do nowadays; and you employ it at your peril. In this crowded and hurried reading age, pages that require such close attention remain unread and neglected. You can't skip a word if you are to get the effect, and 19 out of 20 worthy readers grow intolerant. The method seems perverse: "Say it *out*, for God's sake," they cry, "and have done with it".[22]

William was, of course, fifteen months older than Henry and it is well-known that the younger brother had a perfectly conscious life-long feeling that he would never be able to catch up:

> At Cambridge of course, when I got there, I was further to find my brother on the scene and already at a stage of possession of its contents that I was resigned in advance never to reach; so thoroughly I seemed to feel a sort of quickening savoury meal in

---

[21] Edith Wharton, *A Backward Glance*, 177-78.

[22] *The Letters of William James*, II, 277-78.

any cold scrap of his own experience that he might pass on to my palate.[23]

Even without Henry's own statement that he was a "timorous" child, in adolescence "anxiously mute"[24], it is not difficult to extrapolate from the observed adult personalities of the brothers — William "is simpler and full of enthusiasms and freshness, whereas Henry is jaded and reticent"[25] — and to see with what scorn and impatience an energetic and voluble William must have superintended the halting early articulations of his younger companion. (Edward Emerson, the family friend, gives the interesting impression that Henry's characteristic family pose was silence.) Now I am not implying that Henry suffered early traumatization by William's easier accomplishments: only that William witnessed Henry's early difficulties and on some level remembered them. It remains for us to reach some understanding of why Henry developed and preserved an inability to "say out" his thoughts and feelings. The special importance of *The Turn of the Screw* in James's psychical history is precisely that it enables us to make this reconstruction.

The last chapter of the story traces the steps that lead to the death of little Miles. It is, in my view, important to see two things: first, that these steps are distinct and definite; and second, that the story stops abruptly with the child's death. The question why Miles dies is, of course, a famous puzzler in the criticism and theories abound : the exorcism of Quint has left the child bereft of the will to live; the governess has frightened (or perhaps squeezed) him to death; or what you will. The fact remains, however, that, if we read literally, Miles dies as a result of speaking certain words that have remained unsaid up to that point. And when he has said them everything stops dead. This is what I meant when I alluded to the distinct and definite steps that led to his death. These are none other than the steps that the governess takes to make him "say out" the words around which he has "sighed and

---

[23] *Autobiography*, 417-18.

[24] *Ibid.*, 317.

[25] *Henry James at Home*, 128.

breathed" for some time. The steps are those in the governess's interrogation of the child.

Let us not forget that, even setting aside the extravagantly tortuous — reluctant — dialogue of the piece, the theme of forbidden words has permeated the story from the beginning. The governess is forbidden to contact her employer ("Not a word. I'm off!"); a letter reporting Miles's offence at school lies for a time unopened; opened, that letter merely alludes to "something" and is promptly locked away; the child, finally questioned, discloses it was a question of "things [he] said", only to "those [he] liked".[26] And it is finally the governess's question, the first direct exigent question of the story, that brings down the house. It needs no Freud to conclude that an anxiety focussed on the power or effect of speech is deeply rooted in James's story.

It is necessary to be quite clear about the exact timing of Quint's appearances in the closing sequence. He appears precisely at the moments when the governess broaches the murky issue of the Miles's offence at school and is requiring the child to speak. Note the perfect impasse of the situation: she requires him merely to report — as if in some innocuous metalanguage — the forbidden words but provokes "instead" a speaking of them as Miles is coerced to the naming aloud of Quint. It is at this point that the child dies, destroyed — it seems — by the words that he knew not to say and by the governess's sadistic insistence on speech.

What are we to make of this fatal misalliance? What is the buried wisdom of Miles's refusal to speak, of the anxious muteness he shares with his younger creator? As we have already noted, throughout the story, Peter Quint has nothing to say. More precisely, a strict silence is the very medium in which he appears — with this crucial addition: that Quint's presence is actually productive of an awful hush — sound dies before him:

> It was as if, while I took in, what I did take in, all the rest of the scene had been striken with death. I can hear again, as I write, the intense hush in which the sounds of evening dropped. The rooks stopped cawing in the golden sky and the friendly hour

---

[26] *The Turn of the Screw*, 10, 87.

lost for the unspeakable minute all its voice. But there was no other change in nature, unless indeed it were a change that I saw with a stranger sharpness.[27]

It seems to me that Quint's presence is to be understood as an exhortation to silence: he always has the force of this specific interdiction. And here we arrive at the heart of the early "speech neurosis" of Henry James. James's early and persisting inhibition of speech — his stammer, his hesitations, his silence — marks a disturbance in the verbal sphere caused by a feeling of imminent danger — a danger that threatened if, for example, forbidden words were said out. That his father was the original embodiment of this danger we can infer from the child's evident assumption of the defence of identification, for Henry Senior had a stammer. But it is above all the pressure of oral sadistic fantasies contaminating the verbal sphere that invests spoken words with such imagined destructive power. It is not without significance that, as I noted in opening, *The Turn of the Screw* was the first dictated story and that James tried to frighten his male amanuensis as he composed aloud.[28] Naturally, these things must also be brought into connection with the investigations of my second chapter. As we noted there, it cannot reasonably be considered coincidence that James's dictation era was also the era of his guilty and troubled "Fletcherism", the chewing madness that dogged him for many years. But if oral licence meant danger, silence meant the avoidance of destruction, perpetrated or suffered; and it is just such a failure to be silent that ends *The Turn of the Screw*.

In all these things it is important to see that we are considering the childhood precursors of the extraordinary verbal style of James's maturity — the style that, significantly, only fully became itself when James created by dictation, by saying. What must he do in dictation but — in the unconditional space of imagination — "say out" whatever comes into his head. *He cannot do it*: he has no such facility. The baffling labyrinth of the mature style is in

---

[27] *Ibid.*, 16.

[28] *Ibid.*, 178.

essence a compromise-formation:[29] it represents the uneasy misalliance of a ferocious oral drive with a powerful inhibition on the discharge of that energy, by saying out, for example. (In *The Turn of the Screw* this corresponds precisely with the governess's rage to say, on the one hand, and Miles's reluctance to speak on the other.) And the style's fusion of a powerful drive energy with an ineradicable habit of lexical and syntactical evasiveness is not only a derivative of instinctual conflict: as an act of the mouth, it remains embedded in the primitive material of that conflict. "Kind and elaborate as ever" a visitor of 1911 says of the ageing novelist.[30] The whole issue lies also in this often-noted "elaborate" ceremonial of kindness and courtesy that James used with his guests. Elaborateness mediates his approach to his objects, his hesitations shield them. By 1911 it is an old story.

If Quint's appearance is, then, a kind of paternal exhortation to silent obedience, it is also — as the quotation above clearly illustrates — the determinant of a change in the modality of experience from hearing or speaking to vision. What you cannot say you may "look". Quint both silently "fixes" his objects and elicits acts of looking. We can say therefore that the drive energy which is checked in the oral-verbal sphere is deflected into the visual sphere. And here we rejoin by another route our earlier view of Quint as one who hunts with his eyes.

"When I go to Europe again it will be, I think, from inanition of the eyes" announces the young Henry James to a correspondent in 1870.[31] This image falls gracefully from the pen of one whose verbal invention is so free and copious that it is easy to admire the youthful *jeu d'esprit* and proceed without further thought. But James's cleverness here sports with an image that is tellingly characteristic, for his prose is littered with phrases that associate

---

[29] *The Language of Psychoanalysis*, 76.

[30] *Henry James at Home*, 128.

[31] *Life*, I, 286.

food and sight. Such images are worth investigating, partly because they will help us further to anatomize Peter Quint and partly because (which is the same thing) they cover and mark the site of a Jamesian fixed idea. It is not difficult to turn up examples. In the Hawthorne book of 1879, James can lament "the lightness of diet to which the great Romancer's observation was condemned", despite his "appetite for detail". Elsewhere, Hawthorne is "hungry for the picturesque", of which there is, however, no "copious provision".[32] A letter of 1873 finds James anxious to share his feast of Roman memories with his brother, since otherwise he may "swallow [his] impressions like a greedy feeder".[33] Four years earlier, a letter to his sister Alice represents him as spending his mornings in the Vatican and his afternoons strolling

> at hazard, seeking what I might devour and devouring ... whatever I have found.[34]

A letter of 1870 finds a repatriated James expressing his enthusiasm for

> a number of Siennese photos, which I have literally devoured. My brother says that to him, for several days, they have been as meat and drink.[35]

In general, repatriation breeds "hungry Eastward thoughts" of the Europe to which he will return for sustenance, for in Cambridge "his sense aches at times for richer fare".[36]

Now while it is undeniably true that the spirit of most of these remarks is self-consciously sportive, their humour by no means disqualifies them from psychic significance. It is difficult to avoid

---

[32] *Hawthorne: Henry James*, ed. Tony Tanner, London, 1967, 54, 73.

[33] *Letters*, I, 321.

[34] *Ibid.*, 163.

[35] *Ibid.*, 243.

[36] *Life*, I, 286.

the suspicion that, in this playful fusion of visual and oral imagery, we have an important adult derivative of the early internal history that we have been attempting to reconstruct. If, at the time of the acquisition of speech, Henry James indeed suffered a deflection of drive energy into the visual sphere, the evidence of this food-sight imagery once again suggests that a predominance of oral sadism primarily determined that deflection and its character. On the secondary level, there is good reason to suppose that the agency of sight was chosen both on account of Henry's visual acuity and the weakness of father's sight, and William's. There is no doubt whatsoever that, not merely in *The Turn of the Screw*, but in Henry's fiction generally, the ego function of looking inherits a sadistic colouring and is frequently represented in oral terms; neither can it be doubted that the associated instinctual pressure was such that James suffered an extraordinary hypertrophy of the scoptophilic instinct. All of this finds powerful representation in the fiction. In *The Sacred Found* (1901), for example, the cannibalistic curiosity of the narrator leads him to this culpable feast of scrutiny:

> My question had not been in the least intended for pressure, but it made her turn and look at me, and this, I quickly recognised, was all the answer the most pitiless curiosity could have desired .... Beautiful, abysmal, involuntary, her exquisite weakness simply opened up the depths it would have closed. It said everything, and by the end of a minute my chatter ... was hushed to positive awe by what it had conveyed. I saw as I have never seen before what consuming passion can make of the marked mortal on whom, with fixed beak and claws, it has settled as on a prey .... Voided and scraped of everything, her shell was merely crushable.[37]

This means that when James creates a Quint who (permitted his creator's preferred term) "fixes" his objects in a deathly gaze after "prowling for [that] sight", the imagery employed is far from casual. It is dictated by internal processes of infantile origin. Extrapolating to later (Oedipal) development, we might say that, after the defeat of his phallic aspirations (the "wound"), Quint has

---

[37] Henry James, *The Sacred Fount*, New York, 1901, 135-36.

(regressive) recourse to a king of substitute virility of sight. The "awful bloody beak" of "vindictive intention" that — allied, inevitably, to the issue of "looking" — finds its way, eighteen years later, into the deranged deathbed dictations of Quint's creator, serves only as an additional last confirmation of the powerful oral-sadistic character of the drive energy with which the act of looking became invested in the course of James's development.[38]

If we have now constructed a more satisfactory account of Peter Quint, one that, acknowledging his weakness, can nevertheless attempt to explain his powerful presence, we have still not arrived at a balanced reading of the story. For the governess of this account has up to now figured as the more or less passive victim of the ghostman, condemned to frustrations of which he is the author. Certainly, there is much in her portrait — and much in the tradition of governesses out of which she rises — to sustain such a view: she is young, she is poor, she is "untried".[39] But in the struggle between herself and Quint, it is far from accurate to propose her as a dramatically less vigorous combatant. It turns out, indeed, that the very question that has occupied us to this point — that of what we may call Quint's potency — is not unrelated to the nature of his adversary. The nameless heroine has her own formidable intensity, and an understanding of the place of that quality in the scheme of the story will provide a crucial last turn to the screw of our investigation.

We must return to the appearances of Peter Quint, no longer now to demonstrate their iterative and unchanging characteristics, but, on the contrary, precisely to see what changes in them. For they do change, though not in essence because Quint does, but rather because the governess presses herself in a particular direction, struggles to assume a particular position, and this is duly reflected in her remorselessly developing relation to the dead valet. That Quint does not change, that he, from first to last —

---

[38] *Letters*, IV, 810.

[39] *The Turn of the Screw*, 6.

for all the intensity of his stare — seems trapped and immobile in his silent and essentially excluded part, this circumstance seems in the end but an additional commentary on the governess's development and indeed a strict complement to that development.

She sees him first — her adversary — on the crenellated tower as she walks beneath in the gardens of her new home. Like her Harley Street employer, the elevated stranger "rises" before her, marking a distance that seems like an interdiction.[40] We need not return to the fear conjured up in her. What our second scrutiny of the scene selects instead is a thought that flits through her mind: that the figure her imagination — she admits — half expected seems not most "in place" at "such an elevation".[41] Accordingly, Quint is indeed never again encountered in a setting that flatters and aggrandizes as this first does. When she next meets him, he has descended to the ground level where she herself stands. (He will never rise again.) He is, we recall, outside the dining-room window, looking in as the governess looks out. Her (reiterated) insistence that he is "the same" does not prevent a crucial modulation: no longer fixed to the spot, she fairly "bounds" out of the house:

> It was confusedly present to me that I ought to place myself where he had stood. I did so; I applied my face to the pane and looked, as he had looked, into the room. As if, at this moment, to show me exactly what his range had been, Mrs Grose, as I had done for himself just before, came in from the hall. With this I had the full image of a repetition of what had already occurred. She saw me as I had seen my own visitant; she pulled up short as I had done; I gave her something of the shock that I had received. She turned white, and this made me ask myself if I had blanched as much.[42]

---

[40] *Ibid.*, 4.

[41] *Ibid.*, 16.

[42] *Ibid.*, 21.

Here we find ourselves again on what was, psychically speaking, familiar terrain to Henry James, essentially the terrain, *mutatis mutandis*, of his dream of the Louvre. As in the dream, an assailant, a "visitant", pressing inward, is himself put to flight by his would-be victim.[43] And there could be no clearer indication of the mechanism of defensive identification involved in that rout. The governess's fear is mastered by a literal assumption of Quint's place and with it his attendant fearsomeness. And that this — impressively *active* — reversal yields fruit not merely delusive, becomes perfectly clear when one considers the governess's next encounter with Peter Quint.

Since this happens inside the sleeping house, it is again, in appearance, a question of a "forward stride in our intercourse".[44] But this is a phrase that, to attuned ears, is redolent of the simple irony that Quint, while persevering, is now essentially in retreat, and is perhaps, indeed, never other than at bay, like some "baffled beast".[45] We recall that this (first and last) indoors confrontation is on a darkened stairwell on which, as the governess stands *above*, Quint stealthily ascends. She has had, she informs us, some seconds to "stiffen" herself before the predator sees her, and is able to reflect that

> ... dread had unmistakably quitted me and ... there was nothing in me unable to meet and measure him.[46]

Seeing her, Quint is "stopped short" and they face each other in a "common intensity". In this mutual stare, her stillness perfectly matches that of the ghostman and her identificatory intentness reaches even to matching him in his deadness, as she wonders whether "I were in life". Outfaced, Quint turns and descends. That he had at no point been other than *below* the governess makes this outcome a foregone conclusion. She has usurped the

---

[43] *Autobiography*, 196-97.

[44] *The Turn of the Screw*, 20.

[45] *Ibid.*, 85.

[46] *Ibid.*, 41.

position that was his only at the outset (on the tower) and their subsequent meetings symbolically enact a progressive exchange of power. Readily allied to this are some reflections that, days later, she has on looking down the same stairway, to see the ghostly Miss Jessel seated in a "half-bowed" defeated posture below:

> ... I wondered whether, if instead of being above I had been below, I should have had the same nerve for going up that I had lately shown Quint.[47]

This imaginative revisiting of a feminine position makes perfectly clear the extent to which she has now repudiated that position. It also puts us in the position to offer a further-refined hypothesis as to the most primitive psychical core of the Louvre dream and this fictional recasting of it. In as much as the dream turns on the night terror of a man threatened by the approach of an assailant as he sleeps, it seems reasonable to view the "admirable nightmare"[48] in broadly Oedipal terms, and to find it it a clear expression of a castration anxiety. But the genetic precursors of the phallic and castrated opposition of the Oedipal level of conflict are the masculine/feminine and active/passive oppositions of earlier development. From this perspective, the dream appears to turn on a masculine repudiation of an imminent intrusion that threatens to produce feelings of intolerable (feminine) passivity. The repudiation is effected primarily by the defence of identification. In essence, what happens in *The Turn of the Screw* is that, in the (profoundly appropriate) imaginative vessel of the "untried" governess, these primitive "feminine" terrors of her creator are summoned up and the history of an attempt to master them is unfolded. Within the tale, this ancient conflict is charted as the governess's struggle with a questionable man, the "actor" Peter Quint, who dresses in the borrowed robes of his Master. In the surreal mobility of the tale's clothing it is not hard to make out a deep suggestiveness. For the essence of the thing is *her* progressive assumption, *her* putting on of this masculinity, and

---

[47] *Ibid.*, 43.

[48] *Autobiography*, 196.

it is towards this end that the whole ferocious endeavour of the tale is directed.

It is, indeed, only when looked at in this way, looked at from the direction of the psychic history of its creator, that the extraordinary ending of *The Turn of the Screw* can be credited with a meaning that surpasses the intellectual or imaginative whims of the individual reader. What can we say of that ending, first of all, that is more suggestive than the fact that the other women (Flora, Mrs Grose) have been driven out of Bly in preparation for the governess's supreme performance? For that performance is intent on nothing other than the expulsion of the feminine from her own nature and the driving out of the others, old woman and child, is a bold preliminary sketch, an already extravagant earnest of what is to come. Alone with Miles — "the little gentleman" who shares his uncle's tailor — she waits for Quint, who does not fail to put in one last appearance. The resultant final contest attains an awesome dramatic intensity; but, to our heightened understanding, Quint is not merely present as the desperate face at the window. The governess has never seemed more ferocious in the rage of her own intentions, never more "blind with victory"[49] than now, as she tries to press the young man to her body and possess his secrets. Out of this frenzied drama of possession looms a sentence that tells us we are close to the end: she "reddens to the roots of [her] hair".[50] Her hair now the colour of Quint's, there can be little surprise in the last sentence that the "little gentleman" has breath to utter:

"Peter Quint — you devil!"[51]

This is the text's most famous ambiguity, the question of whom these words are hurled at — the governess or the visitant outside the window. But Miles has not merely uttered these words: he has made a "supreme surrender of the name" and his dead heart is

---

[49] *The Turn of the Screw*, 87.

[50] *Ibid.*, 86.

[51] *Ibid.*, 88.

shortly to be pronounced "dispossessed".⁵² Quint also has vanished. It is evidently to the governess that the name has been surrended, in her favour that the men have been dispossessed. Psychically speaking, there is no ambiguity in Miles's final tribute to his governess. With these four words her awesome assumption of an imaginary masculinity is complete.

But this is not to say that the climax of her history — the ending of her tale — is unequivocally positive for the governess. For all its savage triumphalism, the closing sequence is shot through with pity and fear. Moreover, from the outset, the story has been offered as that of a woman who is already dead, already entered into the sphere of her strange quarry. This need not surprise us, given her persistent preoccupation with his place. More important, however, is the related recognition that the first (or Quint-centred) sequence of my argument, is not unseated by the second, centred on the governess. For her progressive, self-preservative identification with Quint, is nevertheless with what we have seen as a damaged object — not a "gentleman"⁵³ — rather than with some fuller, more complete embodiment of the active and masculine. In other words, her story ends with a *flawed* solution, and a solution that doubtless opens into the reality of her creator and his earliest identifications.

Having suffered the amputation of his right leg above the knee when he was fifteen, Henry James Senior was, after all, a man physically incomplete. Something of his attitude to that inglorious injury and to the circumstances that occasioned it may be inferred from the fictional shift to which he treats it in his autobiography. There — as in the history of Peter Quint — the injury is to the *upper* man, an arm is lost, and the cause is elevated from a prank to a gunshot.⁵⁴ He had been broken, too, in the first years of his marriage, by the unexpected after-dinner appearance to him of an

---

⁵² *Ibid.*

⁵³ *Ibid.*, 22.

⁵⁴ F. O. Matthiessen, *The James Family*, New York, 1947, 17, 18n.

apparition that was destined to be the prototype of all Jamesian hauntings:

> To all appearance it was a perfectly insane and abject terror, without ostensible cause, and only to be accounted for, to my perplexed imagination, by some damned shape squatting invisible to me within the precincts of the room, and raying out from this fetid personality influences fatal to life. The thing had not lasted ten seconds before I felt myself a wreck; that is, reduced from a state of firm, vigorous, joyful manhood to one of almost helpless infancy. The only self-control I felt capable of exerting was to keep my seat. I felt the greatest desire to run incontinently to the foot of the stairs and shout for help to my wife .... [55]

We have no account of Mary James's view of this or of the two years that her husband needed for the regaining of his mental and emotional equilibrium. But his use of the word "incontinently" in this (1879) account is striking, as is also, given our analysis of *The Turn of the Screw*, the imaginary image of the unmanned young husband hobbling to the foot of the stairs to seek help from his young wife above. There is no doubt at all that Mrs James was a person of considerable self-possession and one whose efficiency in all the offices of external management inclined her to be relatively unsympathetic — if not indeed a little obtuse — to the world of feelings. The long habit of self-sacrifice and selflessness — creating an accumulating (and undischargeable) indebtedness in others — made her view the vivid expression of ("selfish") feeling as weakness. There can be no clearer indication of this than her recorded attitudes to the bowel movements of children. When her first grandchild displayed a tendency to constipation, she could find no cause for anxiety. It was the malady of strong infants: only "the less fine specimens" were likely to be

> troubled the other way [by diarrhoea] — so this is not a weak, but a strong point in the little man — Everything evinces his superiority. [56]

---

[55] Henry James, *Society the Redeemed Form of Man*, Boston, 1879, 43-44.

[56] J. Strouse, *Alice James*, New York, 1980, 24.

There is very little reason for surprise, therefore, that when, for example, in 1874 the *materfamilias* writes to her (frequently constipated) son Henry about his brother William's persistently morbid state of mind, she locates the seat of his trouble in the fact that he "*must express* every fluctuation of feeling".[57] Not for nothing will the reticent mature novelist, wary of first person narration, speak of "the terrible *fluidity* of self-revelation".[58] All of which provides the all-too-evident context within which Father's "incontinently" asks to be read. It formulates Mary's likely view of the extravagance of his after dinner visitation and of his reaction to it: so he must contain himself and display the placid control to which his wife's whole demeanour was an implicit tribute.[59] We will find no incongruence between this state of affairs and certain of the elder Henry's social ideas. Notably, he held that the nature of social and domestic authority was changing in his time from the old paternal and tyrannical style to a style more maternal. This new masculine authority was to be characterized by "the utmost relaxation, indulgence, and even servility".[60] There can be little doubt that mother provided a quietly formidable centre in a household riddled with the father-derived cancer of masculine indecision. True control in the James household resided in the "little buffalo" to whom weak backs, weak eyes, weak nerves, uncertain careers and strong imaginings were unknown.[61]

It seems to me to be a short step from these matters back to *The Turn of the Screw*, where the bewildered protagonist attempts,

---

[57] *Ibid.*

[58] Blackmur, 321.

[59] Remoter family history is impressively repeated in this also. When the teenage amputee was suffering appallingly after the crude unanaesthetized surgery of the day, his father's extravagant displays of emotion had to be checked by his wife. See *The James Family*, 18.

[60] *The Literary Remains of the Late Henry James*, ed. William James, Boston, 1884, 169-70.

[61] Alice James, 25.

for the mastering of her fears, to "take on" one Peter Quint, who represents a deeply questionable ideal of manhood. It is my conviction that Henry James Senior stands (or falls!) behind Peter Quint, primarily as a damaged, overmastered man. But, as if for corroboration of this hypothesis, many other details of the history of Henry James's father are condensed into the portrait of Quint: his early addiction to alcohol, his irregular dissolute life of that same era, his premature return home from "school" — this all ending when his "fall" deprived him of part of his lower body. And, coming at the thing from the other side, it is significantly (as so often in James) in the imaginative vessel of a female protagonist — vulnerable to visitants — that the enterprise of mastery is undertaken. All of which tends to the conclusion that it is in the labyrinth of early (and unsatisfactory) identifications that the innermost meaning of *The Turn of the Screw* is to be sought. But as in analytical treatment, so too in a psychoanalytically-oriented criticism, this is a meaning we must patiently uncover, not invent.

5

The Jameses and Psychoanalysis

> I fancy the pair understanding each other too well — fatally well. Neither can protect the character of the other against itself — for the other in each case is, also, equally the very self against whom the protection is called for .... Two lives, two beings, and *one* experience .... They may be twins, but I don't think it necessary. They needn't even be brother and sister: they may be two brothers or even two sisters .... The dénouement would be: to what that conducts you — conducts the victim. It conducts to a sharing of the fate of the other, whatever this fate may be.
>
> Henry James, *Notebooks*, 5 February 1895.

Freud's visit to New England in the autumn of 1909 marked the beginning of an era: that of the thorough-going introduction of psychoanalysis into the New World. By May 1911, the American Psychoanalytic Society had been formed, and in September of that same year, James Jackson Putnam, distinguished Harvard Professor of neurology — who had been converted to a psychoanalytic way of thinking by his contact with Ernest Jones — attended, and lent his prestige to, the International Congress in Weimar. Among the American audience that, two years earlier, in September 1909, had given its rapt attention to the Clark lectures, delivered by Freud in a relaxed and conversational German, was the then gravely-ailing William James, well enough to be present for only one of the five sessions. He had travelled to Worcester "for one day in order to see what Freud was like".[1] The ideas of Freud were not new to him: a professional psychologist since 1886, William had been the author of a brief notice of the Freud-Breuer "Preliminary Communication" (1893) that appeared in the *Psychological Review* in 1894. William James was accordingly responsible for the first "learned" mention of Sigmund Freud in print in the United States. Already his characteristically sturdy grace of expression is brought to the describing of early analytic ideas, as, for example, when the psychical traumata that underlie hysteria become "thorns in the spirit, so to speak".[2] Although the matured fruit of Freud's momentous collaboration with Josef Breuer was never reviewed in the United States, William (who had excellent German) had probably gone on to read *Studien über Hysterie* (1895), since he mentions Freud's novel and promising treatment of hysteria in his Lowell lectures of 1896, and yokes the names of Freud and Breuer together in a similar context in the Gifford lectures, delivered in Edinburgh in 1901 and 1902, and later famous as *The Varieties of Religious Experience*. In his way, Freud was destined to return the compliment, for in his *Autobiographical Study* (1924), he recalls his 1909 meeting with William James "the philosopher":

> I shall never forget one little scene that occurred as we were on a walk together. He stopped suddenly, handed me a bag he was carrying and asked me to walk on, saying that he would catch me up as soon as he got through an attack of angina pectoris which was just coming on .... I have always wished that I was as fearless as he was in the face of approaching death.[3]

William James died eleven months later, in August 1910, and so was never to witness the achieved installation of psychoanalysis into the United States. It is perhaps appropriate that in his

---

[1] *The Letters of William James*, II, 327.

[2] J.C. Burnham, *Psychoanalysis and American Medicine 1894-1918: Medicine, Science, and Culture*, New York, 1967, 14.

[3] Sigmund Freud, *An Autobiographical Study*, in *The Complete Psychological Works of Sigmund Freud*, XX, 52.

Psychoanalysis and American Medicine 1894-1918, J.C. Burnham dates "the first book about psychoanalysis by an American" at 1911.⁴ But the question of William James's attitude to the new science is nonetheless a worthwhile one, since at the time of his death he had an acquaintance of about seventeen years with some of its early ideas.

If we take as authoritative the testimony of Ernest Jones, Freud's biographer, we are likely to assume that William James had the kind of unbounded enthusiasm and boyish zest for psychoanalysis that he had for many things:

> James, who knew German well, followed the lectures [sic] with great interest. He was very friendly to us and I shall never forget his parting words, said with his arm around my shoulder: "The future of psychology belongs to your work."⁵

But against this account — with its erroneous implication that James was present for all of Freud's lectures — we need to set the following, more guarded, statement, made by James in a letter to Theodore Flournoy on 28 September 1909, one week after Freud's party had set sail for Europe:

> I hope that Freud and his pupils will push their ideas to their utmost limits, so that we may learn what they are. Psychoanalysts can't fail to throw light on human nature, but I confess Freud made on me personally the impression of a man obsessed with fixed ideas. I can make nothing in my own case with his dream theories and obviously "symbolism" is a dangerous method.⁶

His earlier letter to Mary Calkin (19 September 1909) strikes a similar note:

> I strongly suspect Freud, with his dream theory, of being a regular *halluciné*. But I hope that he and his disciples will push it

---

⁴ *Psychoanalysis and American Medicine*, 33.

⁵ Ernest Jones, *The Life and Work of Sigmund Freud*, abridged edition, London, 1962, 345.

⁶ *The Letters of William James*, II, 327.

to its limits as undoubtedly it covers some facts and will add to our understanding of "functional" psychology, which is the real psychology.[7]

These comments make it clear that James had been present on Thursday 9 September for the third lecture, in which Freud had turned to the topic of dreams. In vain Freud's ironically disarming reference to the trepidation with which he approached the question of dream-interpretation "in a country which is devoted to practical aims": William James's native scepticism was not so readily dissolved.[8] That he was now weak and ailing and that it was thus mortally too late for any revolution in his thinking was in truth but one of the things that stood in the way of the kind of conversion that had proved possible for his friend and colleague, James Putnam. For example, we need to remember also that William had never entered on the practice of medicine for which he had qualified and thus lacked the spur of clinical problems that helped to drive Putnam. Larger than this again, however, was the whole question of the divergence of world-view that is strikingly evident in the references above to a Freud obsessed by a single idea. There can be very little doubt that William James was of a tolerant, sceptical and, above all, pluralistic turn of mind. His interest in the spiritual and the supernatural — in what (in Henry's phrase) lay "beyond the laboratory-brain" — constantly tempted him away from a rigid materialism.[9] It is clear that he could not but be troubled by the ambitious monism of psychoanalysis.

But while these general things are clear, the interesting question of what, precisely, William James made of psychoanalysis would, of course, be a decidedly easier one if he had lived for another decade, to see Freud's ideas develop, gain a larger audience and spawn a wider therapeutic practice. Since his period

---

[7] R.B. Perry, *The Life and Thought of William James*, 2 vols, Boston, 1935, II, 123.

[8] Sigmund Freud, *Five Lectures on Psychoanalysis*, in *The Complete Psychological Works of Sigmund Freud*, XI, 33.

[9] "Is There a Life After Death?", in *The James Family*, 614.

of study under Charcot in Paris in 1882 (earlier, let it be noted, than Freud's own[10]), he had developed an interest in hypnosis, and this in itself might dispose him towards sympathy for the early clinical techniques of psychoanalysis, which had of course, briefly, included hypnosis. He had certainly recommended hypnotherapy for Alice in 1891, the year before her death. On the other hand, it is well-known that, in the United States, psychoanalysis has developed along lines distinct from those characteristic of the European and English traditions. It is also clear that it did so right from the traceable American beginnings in the first decade of the twentieth century. Freud's relations with James Jackson Putnam are an illustrative case in point.

On the one hand, Freud was profoundly grateful to Putnam (one of his hosts during the visit of 1909 and responsible, no doubt, for William James's personal introduction to Freud) for lending his energy and immense social, academic and moral prestige to the new cause — a support that was to continue despite considerable pressure, both public and familial, until his death in 1918. But it also has to be recognized that the theoretical differences between Freud and Putnam were immense. More to the point, they were representative of a direction in which American psychoanalysis was to go. These differences had principally to do with a vein of moral optimism that clung to the New Englander's attitudes but which were quite absent in Freud himself and in his fundamentally dark view of human nature. Troublesome above all to such philosophies of daylight was the Freudian unconscious, which Putnam persisted in making the repository of forces more benign and, as it were, more domesticated than Freud was prepared to countenance. For Putnam, the Freudian unconscious was thus "too negative to be fully satisfactory".[11] By this he meant, for example, that unconscious conflict should not provide the only model of mental functioning: with a catholicity belonging to the same tradition as William James, he insisted that what he saw as the positive social instincts of the neurotic were to be encouraged also. Seemingly

---

[10] Edel gets this wrong. See *Letters*, III, 256n.

[11] Paul Roazen, *Freud and His Followers*, London, 1976, 376.

inaccessible to Putnam — and certainly alien to him — was the notion that moral and philosophical imperatives were utterly incommensurate with the instinctual urges of the primary process,[12] that even the "higher man", with his apparent kindness and altruism, resulted from a transformation of instinct. His morals had only a secondary and epiphenomenal status. Putnam never relinquished the dream of irreducible goodness that Freud never managed even to dream. It is in the context of such representative and characteristic differences as these that William James's remarks about psychoanalysis have to be assessed. In the nature of things, remarks made in passing or passages inserted parenthetically are all we have to go on, for there is in James's work no direct or systematic engagement with psychoanalysis. On the other hand, he does say enough to enable us to form a reasonable idea of the limits of his viewpoint.

Appropriately, it is William's best-known and most widely-read work — *The Varieties of Religious Experience* — that casts most light on his view of Freudian ideas. Two places in the text are of special interest. The first is in the opening lecture ("Religion and Neurology") at a point where he is castigating the pretensions of "medical materialism" with its reductive view of mental processes, in particular the fashion

> quite common nowadays among certain writers, of criticizing the religious emotions by showing a connection between them and the sexual life. Conversion is a crisis of puberty and adolescence.[13]

There are at least two things to note here: first, the quintessentially pre-Freudian assumption that the sexual life first awakens (rather than reawakens) at puberty; and second, a basic hostility towards psychological materialism. Now while it is true that Freud abandoned unpublished his early attempt (in *Project for a Scientific Psychology*) to subject his emergent theories to a rigorously neurological and physicalist description, the attempt

---

[12] *The Language of Psychoanalysis*, 339-41.

[13] William James, *The Varieties of Religious Experience*, London, 1960, 33.

was a serious one, and the *Project* contains in embryo many elements of psychoanalytic theory that were later to receive a more psychodynamic description. Moreover, on the level of theory, Freud could never abandon the desire to place his work on a sound biological foundation, for what other foundation could there be for an understanding of mankind that kept the instincts steadily in view? And in the clinical domain, psychoanalysis is unthinkable without a sustained and orienting reference to the intimate physical history of the patient, who is seen as a body as well as a person, as a body-person indeed. In this respect James was, as we have already noted, philosophically opposed to the spirit of Freud's thought.

When we turn to James's equation of sexuality with post-pubertal experience, we must proceed with care. The identification of infantile sexuality is not made in the *Studies in Hysteria* in 1895: and the erroneous seduction theory was to block its path until 1897. Full public formulation does not come until the *Three Essays on the Theory of Sexuality* in 1905, a full three years after James's lectures. On the other hand, while Freud's ideas moved through discernible stages and had to negotiate numerous crises, they constitute an impressively unified body of thought. The early — albeit jointly-authored — treatise on hysteria is no exception to this pattern, as Freud's preface to the 1908 reissue makes clear:

> The attentive reader will be able to detect in the present book the germs of all that has since been added to the theory of catharsis: for instance, the part played by psychosexual factors and infantilism, the importance of dreams and of unconscious symbolism.[14]

It seems to be perfectly clear that William James was not disposed to give these reductive "psychosexual factors" a prominent place in his thinking, and was therefore uncharacteristically inattentive to the "germs" that, as Freud observes, made *Studies on Hysteria* a text of rich promise. He shows, for example, no recognition of the sexual character of intellectual curiosity, even at the moment of

---

[14] Josef Breuer and Sigmund Freud, *Studies in Hysteria*, in *The Complete Psychological Works of Sigmund Freud*, II, xxxi.

asserting that the "entire higher mental" life awakens with the sexual life (at adolescence). And given the precise elaboration that the theory of infantile sexual development was to receive within a few years — the identification of the oral phase of libidinal organization, for example — there is a retrospective irony almost ludicrous in some of the arguments that William employs to advance his anti-sexual, anti-physicalist argument:

> Language drawn from eating and drinking is probably as common in religious literature as is language drawn from the sexual life .... Christian devotional literature indeed quite floats in milk ....[15]

The second passage of particular interest to us in the *Varieties* occurs in the tenth lecture. Here William is discussing "the most important step forward that has occurred in psychology since I have been a student of that science", the "discovery" of that part of human experience that lies outside the habitual "field" of consciousness. I hesitate over a simpler formulation, for "the unconscious" is not William's preferred term, and these pages hold a generous provision of alternatives. So, his subject is at one moment "subliminal regions", at another the "Subliminal", the "extra-marginal", or again the "ultra-marginal", the "subliminal consciousness", or even "subconscious life". Such fluidity of terminology is interesting, for it provides us with a useful clue to the version of the Freudian unconscious that James is prepared to countenance. (Again, the often equivocating ideas of James Putnam may appropriately be called to mind.) William James's "unconscious" is one reluctant to confess itself a region altogether distinct from ordinary consciousness; that is why there clings to his vocabulary a discernible reluctance to to consider this region anything other than an outlying province of consciousness. The issue is far from "academic", for a recognition of the radical otherness of the Freudian unconscious would entail a painful surrender of hegemony on the part of the conscious ego. But even setting such a central consideration aside, in reading these pages in the *Varieties* it is hard to find in William's sturdy formulations any conviction that he is describing a primitive and

---

[15] *The Varieties of Religious Experience*, 33n.

universal region of the human psyche. But, however this may be, he certainly proceeds to a lucid account of this subliminal region's crucial role in the process of symptom-formation in hysteria:

> In the wonderful explorations by Binet, Janet, Breuer, Freud, Mason, Prince, and others ... we have revealed to us whole systems of underground life, in the shape of memories of a painful sort which lead a parasitic existence, buried outside of the primary fields of consciousness, and making irruptions thereinto with hallucinations, pains, convulsions, paralyses of feeling and motion, and the whole procession of symptoms of hysteric disease of body and mind. Alter or abolish by suggestion these subconscious memories, and the patient immediately gets well.[16]

Aside from liberally extending the credit for the crucial insight into the pathogenesis of hysteria of the Freud-Breuer collaboration ("Hysterics suffer mainly from reminiscences."[17]), and, as I noted above, showing no awareness of the (non-pathological) universality of this "underground life", this is, as a formulation of theory, unexceptionable, and likely, even, to provoke the disarming reflection that William James had a clear grasp of what Freud was saying around the turn of the century. Such a conclusion would be unfortunate, for there are in these pages crucial — and, as I take it, quite representative — lapses of understanding. So, for example, James can speak of

> effects, due to "uprushes" into the ordinary consciousness of energies originating in the subliminal parts of the mind.[18]

What perishes with this "originating" is, of course, nothing less than the conception of repression — the dynamic expulsion from consciousness of ideas and feelings intolerable to it. But to James the unconscious exists for the "accumulation of vestiges of sensible experience", which, in that repository

---

[16] Ibid., 235-36.

[17] *Studies in Hysteria*, 7.

[18] *The Varieties of Religious Experience*, 235.

end by attaining such a "tension" that they may at times enter consciousness with something like a burst. It thus is "scientific" to interpret all otherwise unaccountable invasive alterations of consciousness as results of the tension of subliminal memories reaching the bursting-point.[19]

This sounds perilously close to a theory of overcrowding, and, as such, pays scant attention to the important question of the character of any particular "vestige" of experience destined to be "elaborated ... in subliminal regions of the mind". But, above all, William here turns his back on the essential drama of repression: that it operates because a feeling or idea already carries in consciousness — a consciousness that is thus not free, self-transparent and autonomous — the affective charge that dictates its banishment. It is not the consequent process of "unconscious incubation" that in some manner generates the affect; this is determined, not primarily by the nature of the unconscious, but by the prior response of consciousness to what it expelled. Clearly, the great American psychologist made his own necessary adjustments to the new and promising ideas that came to him from Europe. His own theory of consciousness was, after all, characterized by an essential voluntarism and vigorously opposed the passivity of sensationalism. It is not hard to see how the author of *The Principles of Psychology* (1890) — someone for whom "consciousness is at all times a selecting agency" — might have deep philosophical and emotional differences with a creed in which consciousness is reduced to an excluding agency, and is not the certain master in its own household.[20] William James did not ignore psychoanalysis, but it was perhaps essentially alien to his way of thinking. Although he was a man of awesome intelligence, his understanding drew back from making a full engagement with the bleak doctrines of the new science of the mind.

A thorough investigation of the reasons for this "drawing back" lies outside the scope of the present study. But it was certainly not a simple question of irreducible intellectual bias, or

---

[19] Ibid., 236-37.

[20] William James, *The Principles of Psychology*, 2 vols, New York, 1890, I, 284.

of the spirit of the times, as represented by James Putnam, say. William James's hostility to psychoanalysis had to do with his intellectual convictions — but only in so far as these derived from personal conflicts, unconsciously based. The whole issue went to the core of his being. For James only began finally to reach his own characteristic intellectual convictions, the positions that were to serve and support him to the end of his days, as he emerged from the nervous crisis — or "dorsal collapse" as he called it — that had utterly overwhelmed him in his twenty ninth year, in the opening days of 1870. (This is the crisis that a famous passage in *The Varieties of Religious Experience* later attributed to an anonymous correspondent.) As he began to recover in the spring of that year, his diary (29 April) announces that "yesterday was a crisis in my life". The reader who expects, reading on, to come on something intensely private is likely to be surprised. What follows is a tentatively joyful account of his nascent ability to believe in freedom of the will, a conviction about this possibility stealing over him and raising his troubled spirits:

> My first act of free will shall be to believe in free will.[21]

There is something touchingly self-creative in this simple formulation, this precious straw by which he manages to draw himself up from the Slough of Despond. But to derive such near-miraculous comfort from a mere idea is only possible if the idea represents something other than an intellectual position. What crisis made such a solution possible?

The vivid (anonymous) account of the events of 1870 that William James set down thirty years later in his Gifford Lectures at the University of Edinburgh, tells us that an overwhelming "panic fear" swept over him as he

> went one evening into a dressing room in the twilight to procure some article that was there; when suddenly there fell upon me without any warning, just as if it came out of the darkness, a horrible fear of my own existence. Simultaneously there arose in my mind the image of an epileptic patient whom I had seen in the asylum, a black-haired youth with greenish skin, entirely idiotic, who used to sit all day on one of the benches, or rather

---

[21] R.W.B. Lewis, *The Jameses: A Family Narrative*, London, 1991, 204.

shelves against the wall, with his knees drawn up against his chin, and the coarse gray undershirt, which was his only garment, drawn over them inclosing his entire figure. He sat there like a sort of sculptured Egyptian cat or Peruvian Mummy, moving nothing but his black eyes and looking absolutely non-human. This image and my fear entered into a species of combination with each other. *That shape am I*, I felt, potentially. Nothing that I possess can defend me against that fate, if the hour for it should strike for me as it struck for him. There was such a horror of him, and such a perception of my own merely momentary discrepancy from him, that it was as if something hitherto solid within my breast gave way entirely, and I became a mass of quivering fear. After this the universe was changed for me altogether. I awoke morning after morning with a horrible dread in the pit of my stomach, and with a sense of the insecurity of life that I never knew before. It was like a revelation; and although the immediate feelings passed away, the experience has made me sympathetic with the morbid feeling of others ever since. It gradually faded, but for months I was unable to go out into the dark alone.[22]

It goes without saying that such a crisis did not come from nowhere. (Even the retelling of this tale in a public and academic setting seems to raise strange ghosts in William, as the fearsome and bloody imaginings that close the lecture testify.) In fact, the passage itself alludes to two of the likely antecedents of the crisis. At the beginning of the account, the "sufferer" tells us that, at the time of the attack, he was in a state of "philosophic pessimism and general depression of spirits about my prospects". In addition, a footnote directs the reader — "for another case of fear equally sudden" — to one of the books of his father. The reference is to Henry Senior's 1879 account of his own well-publicized "vastation" at Windsor in 1844, when an after-dinner well-being and cheerfulness suddenly dissolved before a "perfectly insane and abject terror" without apparent cause,

> and only to be accounted for, to my perplexed imagination, by some damned shape squatting invisible to me within the

---

[22] *The Varieties of Religious Experience*, 166-67.

precincts of the room, and raying out from his fetid personality influences fatal to life.[23]

Let us begin with the worries about his "prospects" that preceded William's breakdown. Unquestionably, William James did not move into what was to be his adult career (as an academic psychologist) with anything resembling decisiveness. The year from 1859 to 1860 saw a flirtation with painting that his father countenanced but disapproved, favouring as he did a scientific training for his eldest son. William's subsequent period of study at Harvard Medical School was variously interrupted — notably by the Brazilian scientific expedition with the zoologist Agassiz, though he rapidly became disillusioned with the explorer's life. Here, as with painting, he despondently concluded that he could accomplish nothing that would measure up to what greater men had already achieved. He completed his medical degree but never practised. The breakdown of 1870 came six months after graduation, just as earlier nervous troubles (1861) had followed the abandonment of painting.

It is important to trace father's unmistakable hand in all of this. The elder Henry's cardinal pedagogic principle was that his "boys" [sic] should preserve an essential openness to life's experiences, that the assiduous cultivation of a particular activity or career was undesirable, since likely to be narrowing and limiting:

> I desire my child to be an upright man, a man in whom goodness shall be induced not from mercenary motives as brute goodness is induced, but by love for it or a sympathetic delight in it. And inasmuch as I know that this character or disposition cannot be forcibly imposed upon him, but must be freely assumed, I surround him as far as possible with an atmosphere of freedom.[24]

What sounds like a parental regime admirably liberal implies, of course, its own invisible tyranny, a tyranny of freedom, so to speak. One of its faces was the elder Henry's well-nigh

---

[23] *The Jameses: A Family Narrative*, 51.

[24] Ibid., 79.

pathological restlessness and experimentalism. He was a man who moved house or changed continent as readily as another might change his shirt. This high-minded fadishness made his children's education and early life resemble that of rootless if rather superior gypsies. It is certainly not difficult to see father's philosophy of freedom and his endless peregrinations (that displayed, in Henry's later word, "the impression of aimless vacillation") replayed in William's disabling indecisiveness when it came to choosing something, some line for himself. But William's crisis of 1870 was not essentially a repetition of what had happened to father, though the elements of identification in his make-up are clear enough. Just as the solution to the crisis was the belief — the discovered possibility of believing — in free will, so the essence of the crisis was the stricken feeling of having no self that did not bear the tangible impress of father. So father's crisis is repeated, not as itself, but as a harrowing exemplary instance of what it is to be father's son, that realization yielding also the essential image of the nervous attack — that of a man reduced to a neuter (symbolically castrated) state of passivity and inertia:

> *That shape am I*, I felt, potentially. Nothing that I possess can defend me against that fate, if the hour for it should strike for me as it struck for him. There was such a horror of him, and such a perception of my own merely momentary discrepancy from him .... [25]

Father had emerged from his Windsor vastation to a self-surrender before the beneficence of the deity. From his crisis William James emerged clutching a simple principle and a simple conviction that was destined to serve as the cornerstone of his intellectual life. A man's free acts are possible and they can make a difference, however modest, in the vast scheme of things. A man can be an agent rather than a "neuter". William's resulting life-long emphasis on courage, on free will, and on acts of freedom was the intellectual and emotional fruit of his psychically imperative need to wrest activity from his passive relation to

---

[25] See note 22 above. There is surely more than a glance here at father's missing limb.

father.²⁶ His core position was, accordingly, the very opposite of father's philosophy of self-surrender. Moreover, the word of freedom did not suffice: freedom must prove itself possible as an act:

> My first act of free will shall be to believe in free will.²⁷

The idea of free will (and the act of thought that the idea implied, for "the knower is an actor") was the thread leading out of the labyrinth because it was *not father*.²⁸ Psychoanalysis, on the other hand, *was* father, for it dealt in an epiphenomenal ego whose autonomy was always questionable and always in doubt. The ego of psychoanalysis was not the master of the psychical household. That is why William had to set his face against it and served instead the courageous self-reliance that, ironically, Sigmund Freud so admired in him on that single day when their earthly paths crossed.

Unlike his brother William, Henry James never met Sigmund Freud, nor is there any evidence that he had read Freud's work in English or in German. Just as disappointingly, there is also no epistolary, notebook, or even anecdotal evidence that Henry and William had ever discussed psychoanalysis. The novelist's closest personal approach to Freud was, in fact, that — as we have seen — in the winter following the death of William, his depressed state drove him to seek the help of James Jackson Putnam, who had, of course, been a close friend and colleague of his late elder brother. These early occasional psychoanalytic sessions in Marlborough Street, Boston, extended into the Spring of 1911. In the same period, and as late as April 1911, James also had frequent consultations with Dr Joseph Collins, a New York neurologist

---

²⁶ For an exploration of this area of psychoanalytic thinking, see above all R.R. Greenson, "The Struggle against Identification", *Journal of the American Psychoanalytic Association*, II/2 (April 1954), 200-17.

²⁷ *The Jameses: A Family Narrative*, 204.

²⁸ *Ibid.*, 206.

with a fashionable practice. At the end of July, Henry set sail for England where he was to flee the intolerable solitude of Lamb House for the bustling distractions of London. It was on 4 January 1912 that he wrote to Putnam thanking him for his "last winter's great sympathy" and conveying a ponderous account of his generally improved condition.[29]

We have already considered part of the unconscious subtext of this letter and its possible relation to Henry's natural rivalry with William. (In the same important associational field, it is also worth noting Henry's laboured account of his eating habits to which I have been inclined to attach some significance.[30]) But, as the single document that charts for us James's relations with his "analyst", the letter is, on the whole, disappointingly intent upon externals. There are, nonetheless, some details of interest. For example, James has heard that Putnam was "in these parts in the summer" and laments that he, having been in London, was not "here" — in Lamb House — "to receive you". Putnam was, in fact, passing through England no idle tourist (as James seems to suppose), but was on his way to Zurich, to stay at Jung's villa. There he was to meet up with other psychoanalytic luminaries, before proceeding to Weimar for the International Congress at which he was to deliver the opening paper, on 21 September 1911. Assuredly, Henry James had entered Putnam's life at a significant and dramatic time so far as the latter's relationship with psychoanalysis was concerned, though of all this he appears to have had little, if any, awareness. For the letter also makes innocent reference to the novelist's last consultations with Joseph Collins in New York. In fact, this remark amounted to a significant social and professional *faux pas*. At a stormy meeting of the American Neurological Association in May 1910, Joseph Collins had made a venomous personal attack on Putnam for aligning himself (in the paper he had just delivered) with "Freudism" and its "pornographic stories about pure virgins".[31] In

---

[29] *Letters*, IV, 595.

[30] See above, 22ff.

[31] *The Life and Work of Sigmund Freud*, 386.

these colourful circumstances, Henry's professional frequentation, less than a year later, of Collins *and* Putnam can scarcely have endeared him to the latter, though Putnam was evidently too much of a New England gentleman to make it an issue with his patient. But we must also conclude that, in the world of early psychoanalytic politics, Henry James steered a rudderless and starless course now that William was dead.[32]

But whatever may have been the limitations of James's personal acquaintance with psychoanalysis, or his scant awareness of the controversies that surrounded it in the last decades of his life, we are still left with an impressive fact. Both in his fiction and his life Henry James often displayed an understanding of human behaviour that one feels tempted to call "psychoanalytic". We have seen how imperfectly the concept of repression had graven itself upon William's understanding of psychopathology. Yet in a story that his less scientific brother published as early as 1884, "The Author of Beltraffio", the concept of psychical defence is given a clear fictional embodiment, as a bereaved father turns away from the loss of his child into the "absolute negation of the matter to himself".[33] This is as fine a description of the defence of denial as one could wish.[34] Moreover, the idea of the unconscious is commonplace in James, as is his relatively subtle understanding of it. For example, his references (in 1896 and 1909) to the "deep well of unconscious cerebration" clearly credit the unconscious with structure and purposive activity, allow it to be a process and not some base repository for the detritus of consciousness.[35]

But it was perhaps in his relationship with his talented and ailing sister Alice that Henry came closest to demonstrating a

---

[32] For Collins's conclusions about his patient, see Edel's Life, II, 729 and below, 101.

[33] *Henry James: The Figure in the Carpet and other Stories*, ed. Frank Kermode, Harmondsworth, 1986, 107.

[34] *The Language of Psychoanalysis*, 261-63.

[35] Blackmur, 23.

psychoanalytic understanding of mental processes. All of the James children showed psychoneurotic tendencies to a greater or lesser degree: but it was in Alice that this paternal legacy of a predisposition to neurosis was written in boldest letters.[36] The visitations of "nervousness" that Henry (and William, up to the time of his marriage in 1878) knew intermittently, Alice was familiar with for the whole of her life. Her invalidism became perforce her career and she concentrated herself in it with all the intentness and energy that her brilliant brothers brought to more conventional modes of striving. Only in the last year of her life did an incontrovertible manifestation of organic disease add itself to the array of hysterical and other neurotic symptoms that had long been her companions.[37] Henry's relation to all of this was a close one. After the death of his parents in 1882, he remained with Alice in Cambridge for almost a year. Then, in 1884, Alice in turn crossed the ocean and installed herself in England until her death in 1892. In this period, in which his sister was tended by her female companion and friend, Katherine Loring, Henry was constantly on call and had ample opportunity to observe the curious process of his sister's illness. What did he see?

For one thing, the element of counter-therapeutic perversity in Alice's relations with Katerine did not escape him. He noticed that, if Katherine's presence and ministrations were in intention medicinal, their effect was nevertheless only to confirm Alice in her inveterate prostration:

> I may be wrong in the matter, but it rather strikes me as an effect that Katherine Loring has upon her (she had been up before) and she has now been recumbent ... ever since she reached Bournemouth.[38]

---

[36] This fact deserves a social as well as a psychological commentary.

[37] Alice died from a carcinoma of the breast. See *Alice James*, 301.

[38] *The Diary of Alice James*, ed. Leon Edel, New York, 1964, 12. For related material, see also *Letters*, III, 70.

The thought is not spelt out, but the psychoanalytic concept of secondary gain — often associated with hysterical illness — is clearly present to Henry's remarkable intuition.[39] It was doubtless by recalling his own sickbed experiences, as well as by observing Alice, that he was able to see how those benign and happy concomitants of illness — such as multiplied attention and love — may stealthily insinuate themselves as unconscious aims of the sufferer. ("What are the Patient class but egoistic?" Henry had ruefully asked Putnam.[40]) And the illness, thus succeeding, may perpetuate itself as a ready means to gratification that is otherwise elusive. Illness makes the body an object of uncommon interest to the self and to others, eliciting a familiar ritual of touch and gaze, and above all providing a licence for dependency and regression. So Alice, displacing her epithet, discovers "the most supremely interesting moment in life" when cancer promotes her above the hysteric or neurasthenic.[41] The resultant change in personal aura is not lost on the most observant of men: to William, Henry speaks of

> the serenity of her present attitude, which strikes me, strange as it may appear to you, as a condition of greater *comfort* than she has known for years, or probably *ever* known. The "nervousness" engendered by (or engendering) her intense horror of life and contempt for it is practically falling away from her in view of her future becoming thus a definite and not long — a rapidly *shrinking* term.[42]

But it was two years after Alice's death that Henry arrived at what seems to me his most penetrating insight into her nature. It comes in the remarkable letter he wrote to William (and his wife) on the occasion of Katherine Loring's private publication of Alice's diary. Having expressed delight in the "life, the power, the

---

[39] *The Language of Psychoanalysis*, 182-84.

[40] *Letters*, IV, 597.

[41] *The Diary of Alice James*, 15.

[42] *Letters*, III, 350.

temper, the humour and beauty and expressiveness" of his late sister's "new claim for the family renown", Henry turns to another impression of the diary:

> But it also puts before me what I was tremendously conscious of in her lifetime — that the extraordinary intensity of her will and personality really would have made the equal, the reciprocal life of a "well" person — in the usual world — almost impossible to her — so that her disastrous, her tragic health was in a manner the only solution for her of the practical problem of life ... [43]

It is important to remember in reading this that Henry James is writing in 1894, the year before the publication of *Studies on Hysteria*. Yet his insistence that Alice's nervous illness was not to be understood as a problem *tout court*, but rather as the solution to a problem, is fully and impressively in accordance with emergent psychoanalytic theory. For the varied symptoms and behaviour patterns that characterize psychoneurotic illness do not simply reflect the malfunction of a feeling organism: they attempt a fantastic remedy to a problem that the sufferer can neither solve nor endure without them. James's pre-Freudian thought is not far from the post-Freudian formulation of Sartre:

> ... I consider mental illness the solution that the free organism, in its total unity, invents to be able to live in an unlivable situation.[44]

But the temptation to discover a little Vienna in the head of Henry James must be resisted. It is true that, as he sat with his eccentric sister in her last months and, consenting to become a human cipher, listened calmly and without reproach to the endless agitated outpourings of her small strangled life — it is true that, thus considered, he may take on for us something of the character of an early and near saintly practitioner of the psychoanalytic art. But his insight, however great, inhabited the same human space as the things he could not see. The threshold

---

[43] *Ibid.*, 480-81.

[44] R.D. Laing and D.G. Cooper, *Reason and Violence*, London, 1964, 7.

imposed on his understanding of his sister was precisely his understanding of himself:

> Henry came on the 10th, and spent the day, Henry the patient, I should call him. Five years ago in November, I crossed the water and suspended myself like an old woman round his neck where to all appearances I shall remain for all time. I have given him endless care and anxiety but notwithstanding this and the fantastic nature of my troubles I have never seen an impatient look upon his face or heard an unsympathetic or misunderstanding sound cross his lips. He comes at my slightest sign and hangs onto whatever organ may be in eruption and gives me calm and solace by assuring me that that my nerves are his nerves and my stomach his stomach — this last a pitch of brotherly devotion never before approached by the race. He has never remotely hinted that he expected me to be well at any given moment, that burden which fond friend and relative so inevitably impose upon the cherished invalid. But he has always been the same since I can remember and has almost as strongly as father that personal susceptibility .... [45]

"My nerves are his nerves and my stomach his stomach": there is more in this than a graphic assertion of fraternal love. Behind what was probably, in its original sickroom context, a wittily literal reminder of sympathetic consanguinity, stands a special capacity for identification. For as we have seen, the James children never displayed their symptoms on the *tabula rasa* of illness. From their earliest days, the household constituted a place of psychic fictions, and the family that grew up in it were committed ever after to interpret their lives through this ghostly milieu of imitations and identifications. Considered from a psychoanalytic viewpoint, the Jameses are thus an exemplary instance of what it means to be a family. William once joked that Henry was "a native of the James family" and had no other country. But this was not Henry's fate alone. And it is, if one will, the supreme paradox of the elder Henry's liberal and unfettered regime of education, that children so diverse and brilliant and far-travelled in mind and world were so bound and concentrated and confined in their emotional spaces.

---

[45] *The Diary of Alice James*, 104.

It is this that we must bring to mind as the love-crowned "Henry the patient" suffers with Alice: in the countertransference of the sickroom he *is* Alice — a female body, wounded, ailing, obscurely hurt. Small wonder that, in 1911, Dr Collins concluded that Henry had "an enormous amalgam of the feminine in his make-up", for Alice had long presented an imposing family model of invalidism.[46] No remedy that in her last months the novelist tells William not to be "too much *haunted* with her" and assures himself that he is "less so now than I have been for years".[47] For the repudiation annuls itself in recalling their father's famous "vastation", the *fons et origo* of Jamesian hauntings. At every turn, the family spectres mutter their close and daunting syllogism: "Nothing happens save repetition." So Alice's habit of recumbency — supported by Katherine's presence — is haunted by the amutated father:

> ... there is about as much possibility of Alice's giving Katherine up as of giving her legs to be sawed off.[48]

It goes without saying that Alice continued to haunt her brother from beyond the grave, at least in the paraspectral world of identifications. She takes her place by name in the bizarre family reunion of Henry's deathbed dictation. But she presses close too in the emotional illness that framed the death of William in 1910. The parity of vocabulary is striking: the euphemistic "nervousness", so long Alice's word, is now his own; the clinging terrified dependency on William and his wife, the morbid incapacity to be alone — all this now his.

Alice thus presented Henry with an ideal external means of analysing his own nature, for, in her, many of his own traits were not only present but had been pushed, as if for clearer display, to extremes. There is, however, no evidence that his considerable insights into her neurotic invalidism were ever translated into

---

[46] *Life*, II, 729.

[47] *Letters*, III, 350.

[48] *The Diary of Alice James*, 12.

insights about himself, though, paradoxically, his insight into Alice was certainly facilitated by that very congruity of emotional constitution that he failed to see. Technically speaking, Henry's quasi-analytic relation to his sister failed to take account of the important transference and countertransference elements in that relation: it failed to confront and exorcize the ghosts that mediated their relations to one another and to themselves. For within communication, however rich and free, the unanalysed forms an impermeable membrane, the all-too-human limit of understanding.

But I talk too glibly of failure. Alice once exhorted William not to think of her as "a creature who might have been something else, had neurotic science been born".[49] The creature that Henry James might have been, unburdened of his private demons, is inconceivable to us. In our age, a sanitary house of fiction, open to daylight, can stand only on the lowlands of literature. We must be grateful that our fantastic anatomist was born before neurotic science could have made of *him* a simple body.

---

[49] *Ibid.*, 15.

Appendix

"The Case of George Dedlow" by Silas Weir Mitchell[1]

The following notes of my own case have been declined on various pretexts by every medical journal to which I have offered them. There was, perhaps, some reason in this, because many of the medical facts which they record are not altogether new, and because the psychical deductions to which they have led me are not in themselves of medical interest. I ought to add, that a good deal of what is here related is not of any scientific value whatsoever; but as one or two people on whose opinion I rely have advised me to print my narrative with all my personal details, rather than in the dry shape in which, as a psychological statement, I shall publish it elsewhere, I have yielded to their views. I suspect, however, that the very character of my record will, in the eyes of some of my readers, tend to lessen the value of the metaphysical discoveries which it sets forth.

I am the son of a physician, still in large practice, in the village of Abingdon, Scofield County, Indiana. Expected to act as his future partner, I studied medicine in his office, and in 1859 and 1860 attended lectures at the Jefferson Medical College in Philadelphia. My second course should have been in the following year, but the outbreak of the Rebellion so crippled my father's means that I was forced to abandon my intention. The demand for army surgeons at this time became very great; and although not a graduate, I found no difficulty in getting the place of Assistant-Surgeon to the Tenth Indiana Volunteers. In the subsequent Western campaigns this organization suffered so severely that, before the term of its service was over, it was merged in the Twenty-First Indiana Volunteers; and I, as an extra surgeon, ranked by

---

[1] I reproduce here the original text of Weir Mitchell's story from *The Atlantic Monthly*, XVIII/105 (July 1866), 1-11.

the medical officers of the latter regiment, was transferred to the Fifteenth Indiana Cavalry. Like many physicians, I had contracted a strong distaste for army life, and, disliking cavalry service, sought and obtained the position of First Lieutenant in the Seventy-Ninth Indiana Volunteers, — an infantry regiment of excellent character.

On the day after I assumed command of my company, which had no captain, we were sent to garrison a part of a line of blockhouses stretching along the Cumberland River below Nashville, then occupied by a portion of the command of general Rosencrans.

The life we led while on this duty was tedious, and at the same time dangerous in the extreme. Food was scarce and bad, the water horrible, and we had no cavalry to forage for us. If, as infantry, we attempted to levy supplies upon the scattered farms around us, the population seemed suddenly to double, and in the shape of guerrillas "potted" us industriously from behind distant trees, rocks, or hasty earthworks. Under these various and unpleasant influences, combined with a fair infusion of malaria, our men rapidly lost health and spirits. Unfortunately, no proper medical supplies had been forwarded with our small force (two companies), and, as the fall advanced, the want of quinine and stimulants became a serious annoyance. Moreover, our rations were running low; we had been three weeks without a new supply; and our commanding officer, Major Terril, began to be uneasy as to the safety of his men. About this time it was supposed that a train with rations would be due from the post twenty miles to the north of us; yet it was quite possible it would bring us food, but no medicines, which were what we most needed. The command was too small to detach any part of it, and the Major therefore resolved to send an officer alone to the post above us, where the rest of the Seventy-Ninth lay, and whence they could easily forward quinine and stimulants by the train, if it had not left, or, if it had, by a small cavalry escort.

It so happened, to my cost, as it turned out, that I was the only officer fit enough to make the journey, and I was accordingly ordered to make my way to Block House No. 3, and make the required arrangements. I started alone just after dusk the next night, and during the night succeeded in getting within three miles of my destination. At this time I found that I had lost my way, and, although aware of the danger of my act, was forced to turn aside and ask at a log-cabin for directions. The house contained a dried-up old woman, and four white-headed, half-naked children. The woman was either stone-deaf or pretended to be so; but at all events she gave me no satisfaction, and I remounted and rode away. On coming to the end of a lane, into which I had turned to seek the cabin, I found to my surprise that the bars had been put up during my brief parley. They were too high to leap, and I therefore dismounted to pull them down. As I touched the top rail, I heard a rifle, and at the same instant felt a blow on both arms, which fell helpless. I staggered to my horse and tried to mount; but as I could use neither arm, the effort was vain, and I therefore stood still, awaiting my fate. I am only conscious that I saw about me several Graybacks, for I must have fallen fainting almost immediately.

When I awoke, I was lying in the cabin near by, upon a pile of rubbish. Ten or twelve guerrillas were gathered about the fire, apparently drawing lots for my watch, boots, hat, etc. I now made an effort to find out how far I was hurt. I discovered that I could use the left forearm and hand pretty well, and with this hand I felt the right limb all over until I touched the wound. The ball had passed from left to right through the left biceps, and directly through the right arm just below the shoulder, emerging behind. The right hand and forearm were cold and perfectly insensible. I pinched them as well as I could, to test the amount of sensation remaining; but the hand might as well have been that of a dead man. I began to understand that the nerves had been wounded, and that the part was utterly powerless. By this time my friends had pretty well divided the spoils, rising, together, went out. The old woman then came up to me and said, "Reckon you'd best git up. Theyuns is agoin' to take you away." To this I only answered, "Water, water." I had a grim sense of amusement on finding that the old woman was not deaf, for she went out, and presently came back with a gourdful, which I eagerly drank. An hour later the Graybacks returned, and, finding that I was too weak to walk, carried me out, and laid me on the bottom of a common cart, with which they set off on a trot. The jolting was horrible, but within an hour I began to have in my dead right hand a strange burning, which was rather a relief to me. It increased as the sun rose and the day grew warm, until I felt that the hand was caught and pinched in a red-hot vice. Then in my agony I begged my guard for water to wet it with, but for some reason they desired silence, and at every noise threatened me with a revolver. At length the pain became absolutely unendurable, and I grew what it is the fashion to call demoralized. I screamed, cried, yelled in my torture, until, I suppose, my captors became alarmed, and, stopping, gave me a handkerchief, — my own, I fancy, — and a canteen of water, with which I wetted the hand, to my unspeakable relief.

It is unnecessary to detail the events by which, finally, I found myself in one of the rebel hospitals near Atlanta. Here, for the first time, my wounds were properly cleansed and dressed by a Dr. Oliver Wilson, who treated me throughout with great kindness. I told him that I had been a doctor; which, perhaps, may have been in part the cause of the unusual tenderness with which I was managed. The left arm was now quite easy; although, as will be seen, it never entirely healed. The right arm was worse than ever, — the humerus broken, the nerves wounded, and the hand only alive to pain. I use this phrase because it is connected in my mind with a visit from a local visitor, — I am not sure he was a preacher, — who used to go daily through the wards, and talk to us, or write our letters. One morning he stopped at my bed, when this little talk occurred.

"How are you, Lieutenant?"

"O," said I, "as usual. All right, but this hand, which is dead except to pain."

"Ah," said he, "such and thus will the wicked be, — such will you be if you die in your sins: you will go where only pain can be felt. For all eternity, all of you will be as that hand, — knowing pain only."

I suppose I was very weak, but somehow I felt a sudden and chilling horror of possible universal pain, and suddenly fainted. When I awoke, the hand was worse, if that could be. It was red, shining, aching, burning, and, as it seemed to me, perpetually rasped with hot files. When the doctor came, I begged for morphia. He said gravely: "We have none. You know you don't allow it to pass the lines."

I turned to the wall, and wetted the hand again, my sole relief. In about an hour, Dr. Wilson came back again with two aids, and explained to me that the bone was so broken as to make it hopeless to save it, and that, besides, amputation offered some chance of arresting the pain. I had thought of this before, but the anguish I felt — I cannot say endured — was so awful, that I made no more of losing the limb than of parting with a tooth on account of toothache. Accordingly, brief preparations were made, which I watched with a sort of eagerness such as must forever be inexplicable to anyone who has not passed six weeks of torture like that which I had suffered.

I had but one pang before the operation. As I arranged myself on the left side, so as to make it convenient for the operator to use the knife, I asked: "Who is to give me the ether?" "We have none," said the person questioned. I set my teeth, and said no more.

I need not describe the operation. The pain felt was severe; but it was insignificant as compared to that of any other minute of the past six weeks. The limb was removed very near to the shoulder-joint. As the second incision was made, I felt a strange lightning of pain play through the limb, defining every minutest fibril of nerve. This was followed by instant, unspeakable relief, and before the flaps were brought together I was sound asleep. I have only a recollection that I said, pointing to the arm which lay on the floor: "There is the pain, and here am I. How queer!" Then I slept, — slept the sleep of the just, or, better, of the painless. From this time forward, I was free from neuralgia; but at a subsequent period I saw a number of cases similar to mine in a hospital in Philadelphia.

It is no part of my plan to detail my weary months of monotonous prison life in the South. In the early part of August, 1863, I was exchanged, and, after the usual thirty days' furlough, returned to my regiment a captain.

On the 19th of September, 1863, occurred the battle of Chickamauga, in which my regiment took a conspicuous part. The close of our own share in this contest is, as it were, burnt into my memory with every least detail. It was about six P.M., when we found ourselves in line, under cover of a long, thin row of scrubby trees, beyond which lay a gentle slope, from which, again, rose a hill rather more abrupt, and crowned with an earthwork. We received orders to cross this space, and take the fort in front, while a brigade on our right was to make a like movement on its flank.

Just before we emerged into the open ground, we noticed what, I think, was common in many fights, — that the enemy had begun to bowl round-shot at us, probably from failure of shell. We passed across the valley in good order, although the men fell rapidly all along the line. As we climbed the hill, our pace slackened, and the fire grew heavier. At this moment a battery opened on our left, — the shots crossing our heads obliquely. It is this moment which is so printed on my recollection. I can see now, as if through a window, the gray smoke, lit with red flashes, — the long, wavering line, — the sky blue above, — the trodden furrows, blotted with blue blouses. Then it was as if the window closed, and I knew and saw no more. No other scene in my life is thus scarred, if I may say so, into my memory. I have a fancy that the horrible shock which suddenly fell upon me must have had something to do with intensifying the momentary image then before my eyes.

When I awakened, I was lying under a tree somewhere at the rear. The ground was covered with wounded, and the doctors were busy at an operating table, improvised from two barrels and a plank. At length two of them who were examining the wounded about me came up where I lay. A hospital steward raised my head, and poured down some brandy and water, while another cut loose my pantaloons. The doctors exchanged looks, and walked away. I asked the steward where I was hit.

"Both thighs," said he; "the Doc's won't do nothing."

"No use?" said I.

"Not much," said he.

"Not much means none at all," I answered.

When he had gone, I set myself to thinking about a good many things which I had better have thought of before, but which in no way concern the history of my case. A half-hour went by. I had no pain, and did not get weaker. At last, I cannot explain why, I began to look about me. At first, things appeared a little hazy; but I remember one which thrilled me a little, even then.

A tall, blond-bearded major walked up to a doctor near me, saying, "When you've a little leisure, just take a look at my side."

"Do it now," said the doctor.

The officer exposed his left hip. "Ball went in here, and out here." The doctor looked up at him with a curious air, — half pity, half amazement.

"If you've got any message, you'd best send it by me."

"Why, you don't say it's serious?" was the reply.

"Serious! Why, you're shot through the stomach. You won't live over the day."

Then the man did what struck me as a very odd thing. "Anyone got a pipe?" Some one gave him a pipe. He filled it deliberately, struck a light with a flint, and sat down against a tree near to me.

"Send me a drink of Bourbon."

"Anything else?"

"No."

As the doctor left him, he called him back. "It's a little rough, Doc, isn't it?"

No more passed, and I saw this man no longer, for another set of doctors were handling my legs, for the first time causing pain. A moment after, a steward put a towel over my mouth and I smelt the familiar odor of chloroform, which I was glad enough to breathe. In a moment the trees began to move around from left to right, — then faster and faster; then a universal grayness came before me, and I recall nothing further until I awoke to consciousness in a hospital-tent. I got hold of my own identity in a moment or two, and was suddenly aware of a sharp cramp in my left leg. I tried to get at it to rub it with my single arm, but, finding myself too weak, hailed an attendant. "Just rub my left calf," said I, "if you please."

"Calf?" said he, "you ain't none, pardner. It's took off."

"I know better," said I. "I have pain in both legs."

"Wall, I never!" said he. "You ain't got nary leg."

As I did not believe him, he threw off the covers, and, to my horror showed me that I had suffered amputation of both thighs, very high up.

"That will do," said I, faintly.

A month later, to the amazement of everyone, I was so well as to be moved from the crowded hospital at Chattanooga to Nashville, where I filled one of the ten thousand beds of that vast metropolis of hospitals. Of the sufferings which then began I shall presently speak. It will be best just now to detail the final misfortune which here fell upon me. Hospital No. 2, in which I lay, was inconveniently crowded with severely wounded officers. After my third week, an epidemic of hospital gangrene broke out in my ward. In three days it attacked twenty persons. Then an inspector came out, and we were transferred at once to the open air, and placed in tents. Strangely enough, the wound in my remaining arm, which still suppurated, was seized with gangrene. The usual remedy, bromide, was used locally, but the main artery opened, was tied, bled again and again, and at last, as a final resort, the remaining arm was amputated at the shoulder joint. Against all chances I recovered, to find myself a useless torso, more like some strange larval creature than anything of human shape. Of my anguish and horror of myself I dare not speak. I have dictated these pages, not to shock my readers, but to possess them with facts in regard to the relation of the mind to the body; and I hasten, therefore, to such portions of my case as best illustrate these views.

In January, 1864, I was forwarded to Philadelphia, in order to enter what was then known as the Stump Hospital, South Street. This favour was extended through the influence of my father's friend, the late Governor Anderson, who has always manifested an interest in my case, for which I am deeply grateful. It was thought, at the time, that Mr Palmer, the legmaker, might be able to adapt some form of arm to my left shoulder, as on that side there remained five inches of the arm bone, which I could move to a moderate extent. The hope proved illusory, as the stump was always too tender to bear any pressure. The hospital referred to was in charge of several surgeons while I was an inmate, and was at all times a clean and pleasant home. It was filled with men who had lost one arm or leg, or one of each, as happened now and then. I saw one man who had lost both legs, and one who had parted with both arms; but none, like myself, stripped of every limb. There were collected in this place hundreds of these cases, which gave to it, with reason enough, the not very pleasing title of Stump Hospital.

I spent here three and a half months, before my transfer to the United States Army Hospital for nervous diseases. Every morning I was carried out in an arm-chair, and placed in the library, where some one was always ready to write or read for me, or to fill my pipe. The doctors lent me medical books; the ladies brought me luxuries, and fed me; and, save that I was helpless to a degree that was humiliating, I was as comfortable as kindness could make me.

I amused myself, at this time, by noting in my mind all that I could learn from other limbless folk, and from myself, as to the peculiar feelings which were noticed in regard to lost members. I found that the great mass of men who had undergone amputations, for many months felt the usual consciousness that they still had the lost limb. It itched or pained, or was cramped, but never felt hot or cold. If they had painful sensations referred to it, the conviction of its existence continued unaltered for long periods; but where no pain was felt in it, then, by degrees, the sense of having that limb fell away entirely. I think we may to some extent explain this. The knowledge we possess of any part is made up of the numberless impressions from without which affect its sensitive surfaces, and which are transmitted through its nerves to the spinal nerve-cells, and through them, again, to the brain. We are thus kept endlessly informed as to the existence of parts, because the impressions which reach the brain are, by a law of our being, referred by us to the part from which they came. Now, when the part is cut off, the nerve trunks which led to it and from it, remaining capable of being impressed by irritations, are made to convey to the brain from the stump impressions which are as usual referred by the brain to the lost parts, to which these nerve-threads belonged. In other words, the nerve is like a bell-wire. You may pull it at any part of its course, and thus ring the bell as well as if you pulled at the end of the wire; but, in any case, the intelligent servant will refer the pull to the front door, and obey it accordingly. The impressions made on the cut ends of the nerve, or on its sides, are due often to the changes in the stump during healing, and consequently cease as it heals, so that finally, in a very healthy stump, no such impressions arise; the brain ceases to correspond with the lost leg, and, as *les absents ont toujours tort*, it is no longer remembered or recognized. But in some cases, such as mine proved at last to my sorrow, the ends of the nerves undergo a curious alteration, and get to be enlarged and altered. This change, as I have seen in my practice of medicine, passes up the nerves towards the centres, and occasions a more or less constant irritation of the nerve-fibres, producing neuralgia, which is usually referred to that part of the lost limb to which the affected nerve belongs. This pain keeps the brain ever mindful of the missing part, and, imperfectly at least, preserves to the man a consciousness of possessing that which he has not.

Where the pains come and go, as they do in certain cases, the subjective sensations thus occasioned are very curious, since in such cases the man loses and gains, and loses and regains, the consciousness of the presence of lost parts, so that he will tell you "Now I feel my thumb, — now I feel my little finger." I should also add, that nearly every person who has lost an arm above the elbow feels as though the lost member were bent at the elbow, and at times is vividly impressed with the notion that his fingers are strongly flexed.

Another set of cases present a peculiarity which I am at a loss to account for. Where the leg, for instance, has been lost, they feel as if the foot was present, but as though the leg was shortened. If the thigh has been taken off, there seems to them to be a foot at the knee; if the arm, a hand seems to be at the elbow, or attached to the stump itself.

As I have said, I was next sent to the United states Army Hospital for Injuries and Diseases of the Nervous System. Before leaving Nashville, I had begun to suffer the most acute pain in my left hand, especially the little finger; and so perfect was the idea which was thus kept up of the real presence of these missing parts, that I found it hard at times to believe them absent. Often, at night, I would try with one lost hand to grope for the other. As, however, I had no pain in the right arm, the sense of the existence of that limb gradually disappeared, as did that of my legs also.

Everything was done for my neuralgia which the doctors could think of; and at length, at my suggestion, I was removed to the above-named hospital. It was a pleasant, suburban, old-fashioned country-seat, its gardens surrounded by a circle of wooden, one-story wards, shaded by fine trees. There were some three hundred cases of epilepsy, paralysis, St. Vitus's dance, and wounds of nerves. On one side of me lay a poor fellow, a Dane, who had the same burning neuralgia with which I once suffered, and which I now learned was only too common. This man had become hysterical from pain. He carried a sponge in his pocket, and a bottle of water in one hand, with which he constantly wetted the burning hand. Every sound increased his torture, and he even poured water into his boots to keep himself from feeling too sensibly the rough friction of his souls when walking. Like him, I was greatly eased by having small doses of morphia injected under the skin of my shoulder, with a hollow needle, fitted to a syringe.

As I improved under the morphia treatment, I began to be disturbed by the horrible variety of suffering about me. One man walked sideways; there was one who could not smell; another was dumb from an explosion. In fact, every one had his own grotesquely painful peculiarity. Near me was a strange case of palsy of the muscles called rhomboids, whose office it is to hold down the shoulder-blades flat on the back during the motions of the arms, which, in themselves, were strong enough. When, however, he lifted these members, the shoulder-blades stuck out from the back like wings, and got him the soubriquet of the Angel. In my ward were also the cases of fits, which very much annoyed me, as upon any great change in the weather it was common to have a dozen convulsions in view at once. Dr. Neek, one of our physicians, told me that on one occasion a hundred and fifty fits took place within thirty-six hours. On my complaining of these sights, whence I alone could not fly, I was placed in the paralytic and wound ward, which I found much more pleasant.

A month of skilful treatment eased me entirely of my aches, and I then began to experience certain curious feelings, upon which, having nothing to do and nothing to do anything with, I reflected a good deal. It was a good while before I could correctly explain to my own satisfaction the phenomena which at this time I was called upon to observe. By the various operations already described, I had lost about four fifths of my weight. As a consequence of this, I ate much less than usual, and could scarcely have consumed the ration of a soldier. I slept also but little; for, as sleep is the repose of the brain, made necessary by the waste of its tissues during thought and voluntary movement, and as this latter did not exist in my case, I needed only that rest which was necessary to repair such exhaustion of the nerve-centres as was induced by thinking and the automatic movements of viscera.

I observed at this time also, that my heart, in place of beating as it once did seventy-eight in the minute, pulsated only forty-five times in this interval, — a fact to be easily explained by the perfect quiescence to which I was reduced, and the consequent absence of that constant and healthy stimulus to the muscles of the heart which exercise occasions.

Notwithstanding these drawbacks, my physical health was good, which I confess surprised me, for this among other reasons. It is said that a burn of two thirds of the surface destroys life, because then all the excretory matters which this portion of the glands of the skin evolved are thrown upon the blood, and poison the man, just as happens in an animal whose skin the physiologist has varnished, so as in this way to destroy its function. Yet here was I, having lost at least a third of my skin, and apparently none the worse for it.

Still more remarkable, however, were the psychical[2] changes which I now began to perceive. I found to my horror that at times I was less conscious of myself, of my own existence, than used to be the case. This sensation was so novel, that at first it quite bewildered me. I felt like asking some one constantly if I were really George Dedlow or not; but, well aware how absurd I should seem after such a question, I refrained from speaking of my case, and strove more keenly to analyze my feelings. At times the conviction of my want of being myself was overwhelming, and most painful. It was, as well as I can describe it, a deficiency in the egoistic sentiment of individuality. About one half of the sensitive surface of my skin was gone, and thus much of relation to the outer world destroyed. As a consequence, a large part of the receptive central organs must be out of employ, and, like other idle things, degenerating rapidly. Moreover, all the great central ganglia, which give rise to movements in the limbs, were also eternally at rest. Thus one half of me was absent or functionally dead. This set me to thinking how much a man might lose and yet live. If I were unhappy enough to survive, I might part with my spleen at least, as many a dog has done, and grow fat afterwards. The other organs, with which we breathe and circulate the blood, would be essential; so also would the liver; but at least half the intestines might be dispensed with, and of course all of the limbs. And as to the nervous system, the only parts really necessary to life are a few small ganglia. Were the rest absent or inactive, we should have a man reduced, as it were, to the lowest terms, and leading an almost vegetative existence. Would such a being, I asked myself, possess the sense of individuality in its usual completeness, — even if his organs of sensation remained, and he were capable of consciousness? Of course, without them, he could not have it any more than a dahlia, or a tulip. But with it — how then? I concluded that it would be at a minimum, and that, if utter loss of relation to the outer world were capable of destroying a man's consciousness of himself, the destruction of half of his sensitive surfaces might well occasion, in a less degree, a like result, and so diminish his sense of individual existence.

I thus reached the conclusion that a man is not his brain, or any one part of it, but all of his economy, and that to lose any part must lessen this sense of his own existence. I found but one person who properly appreciated this great truth. She was a New England lady, from Hartford, — an agent, I think, for some commission, perhaps the Sanitary. After I had told he my views and feelings, she said: "Yes, I comprehend. The fractional entities of vitality are embraced in the oneness of the unitary Ego. Life," she added, "is the garnered condensation of objective impressions; and, as the objective is the remote father of the subjective, so must individuality, which is but focused subjectivity, suffer and fade when the sensation lenses, by

---

[2] The original text reads "physical", which is clearly an error for "psychical", as Dedlow is about to describe his *psychological* difficulties.

which the rays of impression are condensed, become destroyed." I am not quite clear that I fully understood her, but I think that she appreciated my ideas, and I felt grateful for her kindly interest.

The strange want I have spoken of now haunted and perplexed me so constantly, that I became moody and wretched. While in this state, a man from a neighboring ward fell one morning into conversation with the chaplain, within ear-shot of my chair. Some of their words arrested my attention, and I turned my head to see and listen. The speaker, who wore a sergeant's chevron and carried one arm in a sling, was a tall, loosely made person, with a pale face, light eyes of a washed-out blue tint, and very sparse yellow whiskers. His mouth was weak, both lips being almost alike, so that the organ might have been turned upside down without affecting its expression. His forehead, however, was high and thinly covered with sandy hair. I should have said, as a phrenologist, Will feeble, — emotional, but not passionate, — likely to be enthusiast, or weakly bigot.

I caught enough of what passed to make me call to the sergeant when the chaplain left him.

"Good morning," said he. "How do you get on?"

"Not at all," I replied. "Where were you hit?"

"O, at Chancellorsville. I was shot in the shoulder. I have what the doctors call paralysis of the median nerve, but I guess Dr. Neek and the lightnin' battery will fix it in time. When my time's out I'll go back to Kearsage and try on the school-teaching again. I was a fool to leave it."

"Well," said I, "you're better off than I."

"Yes," he answered, "in more ways than one. I belong to the New Church. It's a great comfort for a plain man like me, when he's weary and sick, to be able to turn away from earthly things, and hold converse daily with the great and good who have left the world. We have a circle in Coates Street. If it wa'n't for the comfort I get there, I should have wished myself dead many a time. I ain't got kith or kin on earth; but this matters little, when one can talk to them daily, and know that they are in the spheres above us."

"It must be a great comfort," I replied, "if only one could believe it."

"Believe!" he repeated, "how can you help it? Do you suppose anything dies?"

"No," I said. "The soul does not, I am sure; and as to matter, it merely changes form."

"But why then," said he, "should not the dead soul talk to the living. In space, no doubt, exist all forms of matter, merely in finer, more ethereal being. You can't suppose a naked soul moving about without a bodily garment. No creed teaches that, and if its new clothing be of like substance to ours, only of ethereal fineness, — a more delicate recrystallization about the eternal spiritual nucleus, — must not it then possess powers as much more delicate and refined as is the new material in which it is reclad?"

"Not very clear," I answered; "but after all, the thing should be susceptible of some form of proof to our present senses."

"And so it is," said he. "Come tomorrow with me, and you shall see and hear for yourself."

"I will," said I, "if the doctor will lend me the ambulance."

It was so arranged, as the surgeon in charge was kind enough, as usual, to oblige me with the loan of his wagon, and two orderlies to lift my useless trunk.

On the day following, I found myself, with my new comrade, in a house in Coates Street, where a "circle" was in the daily habit of meeting. So soon as I had been comfortably deposited in an arm chair, beside a large pine-table, the rest of those assembled seated themselves, and for some time preserved an unbroken silence. During this pause I scrutinized the persons present. Next to me, on my right, sat a flabby man, with ill-marked, baggy features, and injected eyes. He was, as I learned afterwards, an eclectic doctor, who had tried his hand at medicine and several of its quackish variations, finally settling down on eclecticism, which I believe professes to be to scientific medicine what vegetarianism is to common sense, every-day dietetics. Next to him sat a female, — authoress, I think, of two somewhat feeble novels, and much pleasanter to look at than her books. She was, I thought, a good deal excited at the prospect of spiritual revelations. Her neighbor was a pallid, care-worn girl, with very red lips, and large brown eyes of great beauty. She was, as I learned afterwards, a magnetic patient of the doctor, and had deserted her husband, a master mechanic, to follow this new light. The others were, like myself, strangers brought hither by mere curiosity. One of them was a lady in deep black, closely veiled. Beyond her, and opposite to me, sat the sergeant, and next to him, the medium, a man named Blake. He was well dressed, and wore a good deal of jewelry, and had large, black side-whiskers, — a shrewd-visaged, large-nosed, full-lipped man, formed by nature to appreciate the pleasant things of sensual existence. Before I had ended my survey, he turned to the lady in black, and asked her if she wished to see anyone in the spirit world.

She said, "Yes," rather feebly.

"Is the spirit present?" he asked. Upon which two knocks were heard in affirmation.

"Ah!" said the medium, "the name is — it is the name of a child. It is a male child. It is Albert, — no, Alfred!"

"Great heaven!" said the lady. "My child! My boy!"

On this the medium arose, and became strangely convulsed. "I see," he said, "I see — a fair-haired boy. I see blue eyes, — I see above you, beyond you — " at the same time pointing fixedly over her head.

She turned with a wild start. "Where, — whereabouts?"

"A blue-eyed boy," he continued, "over your head. He cries, — he says, Mamma, mamma!"

Appendix

The effect of this on the woman was unpleasant. She stared about her for a moment, and, exclaiming, "I come, — I am coming, Alfy!" fell in hysterics on the floor.

Two or three persons raised her up, and aided her into an adjoining room; but the rest remained at the table, as though well accustomed to like scenes.

After this, several of the strangers were called upon to write the names of the dead with whom they wished to communicate. The names were spelled out by the agency of affirmative knocks when the correct letters were touched by the applicant, who was furnished with an alphabet upon which he tapped the letters in turn, the medium, meanwhile, scanning his face very keenly. With some, the names were readily made out. With one, a stolid personage of disbelieving type, every attempt failed, until at last the spirits signified by knocks that he was a disturbing agency, and that while he remained all our efforts would fail. Upon this some of the company proposed that he should leave, of which invitation he took advantage with a sceptical sneer at the whole performance.

As he left us, the sergeant leaned over and whispered to the medium, who next addressed himself to me. "Sister Euphemia," he said, indicating the lady with large eyes, "will act as your medium. I am unable to do more. These things exhaust my nervous system."

"Sister Euphemia," said the doctor, "will aid us. Think, if you please, sir, of a spirit, and she will endeavour to summon it to our circle."

Upon this, a wild idea came into my head. I answered, "I am thinking as you directed me to do."

The medium sat with her arms folded, looking steadily at the centre of the table. For a few moments there was silence, then a series of irregular knocks began. "Are you present?" said the medium.

The affirmative raps were twice given.

"I should think," said the doctor, "that there were two spirits present."

His words sent a thrill through my heart.

"Are there two?" he questioned.

A double rap.

"Yes, two," said the medium. "Will it please the spirits to make us conscious of their names in this world?"

A single knock. "No."

"Will it please them to say how they are called in the world of spirits?"

Again came the irregular raps, — 3, 4, 8, 6; then a pause, and 3, 4, 8, 7.

"I think," said the authoress, "they must be numbers. Will the spirits" she said, "be good enough to aid us? Shall we use the alphabet?"

"Yes," was rapped very quickly.

"Are these numbers?"

"Yes," again.

"I will write them," she added, and, doing so, took up the card and tapped the letters. The spelling was pretty rapid, and ran thus as she tapped in turn, first the letters, and last the numbers she had already set down :—

"United States Army Medical Museum, Nos. 3486, 3487."

The medium looked up with a puzzled expression.

"Good gracious!" said I, "they are *my legs! my legs!*"

What followed I ask no one to believe except those who, like myself, have communed with the beings of another sphere. Suddenly I felt a strange return of my self-consciousness. I was reindividualized, so to speak. A strange wonder filled me, and, to the amazement of everyone, I arose, and staggering a little, walked across the room on limbs invisible to them or me. It was no wonder I staggered, for, as I briefly reflected, my legs had been nine months in the strongest alcohol. At this instant all my new friends crowded round me in astonishment. Presently, however, I felt myself sinking slowly. My legs were going, and in a moment I was resting feebly on my two stumps upon thr floor. It was too much. All that was left of me fainted and rolled over senseless.

I have little to add. I am now at home in the West, surrounded by every form of kindness, and every possible comfort; but, alas! I have so little surety of being myself, that I doubt my own honesty in drawing my pension, and feel absolved from gratitude to those who are kind to a being who is uncertain of being enough himself to be conscientiously responsible. It is needless to add, that I am not a happy fraction of a man; and that I am eager for the day when I shall rejoin the lost members of my corporeal family in another and a happier world.

Bibliography

a) Works of Henry James cited

Henry James: Autobiography, ed. F.W. Dupee, London, 1956.

Henry James: Letters, ed. Leon Edel, 4 vols, Cambridge: Mass. and London, 1974-84.

The Tales of Henry James, ed. M. Aziz, 3 vols, Oxford, 1973- .

The Letters of Henry James, ed. Percy Lubbock, 2 vols, London, 1920.

The Art of the Novel: Critical Prefaces, ed. R. P. Blackmur, New York, 1934.

Henry James: Literary Criticism, eds Leon Edel and Mark Wilson, 2 vols, New York, 1984.

Hawthorne: Henry James, ed. Tony Tanner, London, 1967.

The Complete Notebooks of Henry James, eds Leon Edel and Lyall H. Powers, New York, 1987.

Henry James:*The Turn of the Screw*, ed. R. Kimbrough, New York, 1966.

The Golden Bowl, ed. Gore Vidal, Harmondsworth, 1985.

Henry James: Stories of the Supernatural, ed. Leon Edel, London, 1971.

The Sacred Fount, New York, 1901.

Henry James: The Figure in the Carpet and other Stories, ed. Frank Kermode, Harmondsworth, 1986.

b) Other works cited

Abraham, Karl, "A Short View of the Development of the Libido, viewed in the Light of Mental Disorders"(1924), in *Selected Papers of Karl Abraham M.D.*, London, 1927.

Bosanquet, Theodora, *Henry James at Work*, London, 1924.

Brooke-Rose, Christine, *A Rhetoric of the Unreal*, Cambridge, 1981.

Burnham, J.C., *Psychoanalysis and American Medicine 1894-1918: Medicine, Science, and Culture*, New York, 1967.

Derrida, Jacques, *Specters of Marx*, London, 1994.

Edel, Leon, *The Life of Henry James* (revised edn), 2 vols, Harmondsworth, 1977.

Edel, Leon, ed., *The Diary of Alice James*, New York, 1964.

Forster, E.M., *Aspects of the Novel*, London, 1927.

Bibliography

Freud, Sigmund, *The Complete Psychological Works of Sigmund Freud*, 24 vols, ed. James Strachey, London, 1953-74.

Greenson, R.R., "The Struggle against Identification", *Journal of the American Psychoanalytic Association*, II/2 (April 1954), 200-17.

Hayman, Ronald, *K: A Biography of Kafka*, London, 1981.

Hyde, H. Montgomery, *Henry James at Home*, London, 1969.

James, Henry, ed., *The Letters of William James*, 2 vols, London, 1920.

James, Henry [Snr], *Society the Redeemed Form of Man*, Boston, 1879.

James, William, ed., *The Literary Remains of the Late Henry James*, Boston, 1884.

James, William, *The Varieties of Religious Experience* (1902), London, 1960.

James, William, *The Principles of Psychology*, 2 vols, New York, 1890.

Jones, Ernest, *The Life and Work of Sigmund Freud*, abridged edition, London, 1962.

Katan, M., "A Causerie on Henry James's *The Turn of the Screw*", in *The Psychoanalytic Study of the Child*, XVII (1962), 473-93.

Katan, M., "The Origin of *The Turn of the Screw*", in *The Psychoanalytic Study of the Child*, XXI (1966), 583-635.

Laing, R.D. and Cooper, D.G., *Reason and Violence*, London, 1964.

Laplanche, J. and Pontalis, J.-B., *The Language of Psychoanalysis*, trans. D. Nicholson-Smith, London, 1988.

Lewis, R.W.B., *The Jameses: A Family Narrative*, London, 1991.

Matthiessen, F.O., *The James Family*, New York, 1947.

Mitchell, Silas Weir, "The Case of George Dedlow", *The Atlantic Monthly*, XVIII/105 (July 1866), 1-11.

Nunberg, H., and Federn, E., *Minutes of the Vienna Psychoanalytic Society*, 4 vols, New York, 1962-75.

Pawel, Ernst, *The Nightmare of Reason: A Life of Franz Kafka*, London, 1984.

Perry, R.B., *The Life and Thought of William James*, 2 vols, Boston, 1935.

Reed, T.J., *Thomas Mann: The Uses of Tradition*, London, 1974.

Roazen, P., *Freud and His Followers*, London, 1976.

Strouse, J., *Alice James*, New York, 1980.

Wharton, Edith, *A Backward Glance* (1934), London, 1987.

Wilson, Edmund, "The Ambiguity of Henry James", in *The Triple Thinkers*, New York, 1952.

Index

—A—

Abraham, Karl, 26-27
Agassiz, Louis, 96

—B—

Balzac, Honoré de, 3
Beerbohm, Max, 22
Binet, Alfred, 92
Bonaparte, Napoleon, 6, 15-16
Bosanquet, Theodora, 35
Breuer, Josef, 85, 92
Bunyan, John, 54

—C—

Calkin, Mary, 86
Charcot, Jean-Martin, 88
Collins, Joseph, 6, 30, 98-99, 104

—D—

Derrida, Jacques, 57

—E—

Edel, Leon, 15, 19, 49, 51-52
Emerson, Edward, 69

—F—

Flaubert, Gustave, 35, 37
Fletcher, Horace, 23
    Fletcherism, 23-24, 26-27, 31, 71
Forster, E.M., 5
Freud, Sigmund, 4, 18, 26, 31, 64-65, 89-92, 103
    early reactions to, 99
    in America, 84-85, 87-88
    meets William James, 85, 88, 98

—G—

Gosse, Edmund, 22

—H—

Hawthorne, Nathaniel, 2, 73

—J—

James, Alice, 15, 51, 88, 101, 103-105
  "nervousness", 101
  her diary, 102
James, Alice (sister-in-law), 29-30, 51, 105
James, Henry
  "obscure hurt", 40, 42, 64-66
  and his mother, 82
  and psychoanalysis, 98
  deathbed dictation, 15-16, 105
  Louvre dream, 14-18, 25-26, 31-33, 50-51, 54, 77
  verbal eccentricity, 21, 35
James, Henry (works of):
  "A Most Extraordinary Case", 39, 41-49, 55
  "A Tragedy of Error", 20
  "Is There a Life After Death?", 1, 87
  "The Beast in the Jungle", 55
  "The Figure in the Carpet", 8
  "The Jolly Corner", 4, 20, 48-55
  "Theodolinde", 8-14, 24, 27-28
  Hawthorne, 73
  Notes of a Son and Brother, 12
  The Ambassadors, 12
  The American, 4
  The American Scene, 21
  The Awkward Age, 37
  The Golden Bowl, 1-2, 32-33, 36
  The Portrait of a Lady, 4
  The Sacred Fount, 2, 74
  The Turn of the Screw, 9, 27, Ch.4 passim
James, Henry (nephew), 24
James, Henry Snr, 18-19, 30-32, 40, 51, 71, 74, 80, 82-83, 98, 104
  "vastation", 95, 97, 105
  educational theories, 96
  his missing limb, 105
James, Mary, 30, 81-82
James, Peggy, 21-23
James, Robertson, 40
James, Wilkinson, 40
James, William, 2, 8, 15, 18, 20, 22, 24, 27-32, 37, 41, 44, 68, 73-74, 82, 84-102, 104-105
  choice of career, 96
  nervous crisis, 94-98
Janet, Pierre, 92
Jones, Ernest, 84
Jung, Carl Gustav, 99

—K—

Kafka, Franz, 23

—L—

Leavis, F.R., 6, 35
Loring, Katherine, 101-102, 105

—M—

Mann, Thomas, 6
Mitchell, Silas Weir, 38-42

Index

—N—

Noakes, Burgess, 23

—P—

Pinker, James B., 35
Poe, Edgar Allan, 4
Prince, Morton, 92
Psychoanalytic concepts
  activity, 52-54, 77, 79-80, 97
  ambivalence, 27
  castration anxiety, 25, 55, 78, 97
  compromise-formation, 72
  condensation, 58
  conversion (somatic), 67
  countertransference, 104-105
  denial, 100
  displacement, 9, 13, 24, 58, 61, 66
  dream interpretation, 16
  ego function, 74
  externalization, 13, 28
  fixation of libido, 27
  free-association, 28
  genitality, 13, 24
  identification, 16, 71, 77-78, 80, 83, 97, 104-105
  infantile sexuality, 90
  inhibition, 72
  instinct for mastery, 78, 83
  instinctual charge (cathexis), 58, 93
  instinctual conflict, 19, 67, 72, 88
  libido, 13, 24-25, 91
  neurosis, 67, 71, 98-99, 101-103, 105
  oral sadism, 26-27, 71-72, 74-75
  orality, 24-25, 91
  overdetermination, 20, 58
  passivity, 44, 50, 52, 54, 78, 97
  pressure of an instinct, 72, 74
  primary process, 89
  psychical defence, 24, 58, 71, 77-78, 100
  psychical reality, 41, 42
  reconstruction, 69, 74
  regression, 24-25, 27, 45-46, 50, 52, 75
  reparation, 31
  repression, 4, 17, 92-93, 100
  reversal, 28, 32, 77
  scoptophilic instinct, 74
  secondary gain, 102
  sublimation, 34, 47, 64
  the dream-work, 17
  the ego, 58, 91, 98
  the ego-ideal, 16
  the epistemophilic instinct, 90
  the Oedipal, 25, 31-32, 74, 78
  the pre-Oedipal, 28
  the primal scene, 32
  the unconscious, 4, 12, 16, 18, 20-21, 23, 38, 44, 47, 58-59, 61, 64, 88, 91, 93-94, 100, 102
  transference, 105
  unconscious fantasy, 6, 14, 16, 18, 25, 27, 41, 43-44, 63, 65

unconscious thought, 30
wish-fulfilment, 18, 25, 51
Putnam, James Jackson, 6, 30-31, 84, 87-89, 91, 94, 98-99, 102

—S—

Sartre, Jean-Paul, 103

—W—

Wharton, Edith, 1-3, 5, 22, 39, 68
Wilson, Edmund, 5